WILLIAM JENNINGS BRYAN
Golden-Tongued Orator

Every member of Congress was in his place. The gallery was crowded and people stood along the walls and jammed the hallways. William Jennings Bryan was about to speak. He stood tall and strong, a handsome figure, smartly dressed, in western boots.

Everywhere Bryan spoke, excited crowds cheered and applauded. He was called the golden-tongued orator yet he was known as the Great Commoner, fighting for the common people against the power of big corporations and monopolies, fighting against evils in society and government.

Bryan could help even the children in his audiences to understand the big issues. "When you buy one dollar's worth of starch," he said in a farming town, "you pay sixty cents for the starch and forty cents for the trusts and the tariff."

As a schoolboy, Bryan failed to place at all in the first speech contest he entered. Practicing in the fields and woods, speaking with pebbles in his mouth as he heard Demosthenes of ancient Greece had done, planning all year long for upcoming contests, he began to win prizes. While still a youth, he determined to emulate Cicero and use what eloquence and power he might attain, not for himself, but for those who were oppressed. And throughout his life he held to that decision.

A great Christian and a great American, William Jennings Bryan left an indelible mark upon America and upon the world.

William Jennings Bryan

Golden-Tongued Orator

by

Robert A. Allen

illustrated by **Peggy Trabalka**

COPYRIGHT © 1992 by Mott Media, Inc.

Kurt Dietsch, Cover Artist

LIBRARY OF CONGRESS CATALOGING IN PUBLICATION DATA

Allen, Robert A.
    William Jennings Bryan: Golden-Tongued Orator / by Robert Allen; illustrated by Peggy Trabalka.

    p.   cm. — (Sowers series)
    Bibliography: p.
    Includes index.

    SUMMARY: Describes the life of the lawyer, orator, and politician who ran unsuccessfully for the Presidency three times.
    1. Bryan, William Jennings, 1860-1925—Juvenile literature. 2. Statesmen—United States—Biography—Juvenile literature. 3. United States—Politics and government—1865-1933—Juvenile literature. [1. Bryan, William Jennings, 1860-1925. 2. Statesmen.] I. Trabalka, Peggy, ill. II. Title. III. Series: Sowers
E664.B87A45 1991
973.91'092—dc20
[B]
[92]   90-6300
                                                                CIP
                                                                A C

ISBN 0-88062-160-5   Paperbound

CONTENTS

1

"Willy" Bryan and His Family

Young Willy Bryan knew something was wrong by the worried expression on his mother's face. It was the same expression he remembered from that day when he was only three and they had taken little Harry to church in a box and then out to the cemetery where they left him. It was the first thing Willy could remember, and it didn't make any sense to him at the time. Now he was five and he understood a little better what death was all about.

The Civil War had started just one year after he was born. On many evenings people would come to the home of his parents, Silas and Mariah Bryan, sit in their parlor and talk about Silas' favorite subjects, religion and politics—and about the war. It seemed that everyone in Salem, Illinois, knew someone who had died in the war. Though most of the boys from that part of the country were fighting in the Union army, they still had friends from Tennessee, Kentucky, and Missouri whose sympathies were all with the Confederacy. Even Mrs. Lincoln, the wife of the President, who was from Illinois, had three brothers fighting for the Southern cause.

No big battles were fought near Salem, nothing like Gettysburg or Antietam, but Willy overheard enough to know that the war was real. Because they were so close to the states which seceded, many of the Northern sympathizers distrusted anyone who had been a Democrat before the war. They called them "Copperheads" after the poisonous snakes which were commonly found around Salem. Since Mr. Bryan was a Democrat who served for eight years in the Illinois state Senate, he was one of those they did not trust. Many of his friends were arrested and held for weeks without being given a chance to defend themselves in court. Others were taken from their homes during the night and beaten by gangs who called themselves Union Regulators. Their goal was to get all the Democrats to leave the state of Illinois and move south. Although Mr. Bryan did not approve of them, there was also a group called the Knights of the Golden Circle who went around at night shooting and beating Union sympathizers, and burning down some of their homes. It was a dangerous time for everyone.

After supper one night Mrs. Bryan called the children into the parlor as she often did. "It's time for the Bryan Choir to sing," she said, as she took her place at the piano. "Frances, you may choose the first song tonight."

Frances, who was two years older than Willy, chose "When You and I Were Young, Maggie," and then it was Willy's turn.

"May I choose for father, too, since he is not home yet?"

A worried expression crossed Mrs. Bryan's face. It was certainly late for Silas to be out. As judge of the circuit court for six southern Illinois counties, he was always traveling. But on the days when he was able to return home he was seldom gone after dark. Mrs. Bryan forced a smile. "Of course, Willy. Choose one for yourself and one for your father."

"Well, for me I will choose "I'll Go Where You Want Me To Go, Dear Lord," and for father, his favorite, "Kind Words Will Never Die."

"And now, Mother, you must choose," cried Frances when they were finished with Willy's choices. "But please choose 'Farewell, Mother, You May Never Press Me to Your Heart Again.' It's such a sad song and I wanted to choose it myself, but I just had to sing 'Maggie' first. Please, Mother, please?"

Mrs. Bryan smiled indulgently at her three children, Frances, Willy, and little Russell who was still too young to choose a song or even sing with them. There was no way they could know that she sang the sentimental war song as much for the three children she had lost as for them. Virginia and John had both died of whooping cough during the week of Christmas in 1857, and Harry had died just two years before.

They finished the last verse of "Farewell, Mother," and Frances and Mrs. Bryan were wiping away the tears the song never failed to bring. Suddenly they heard a horse trotting into the yard.

"Father's home," shouted Willy, and the Bryan Choir was adjourned for the evening.

Judge Bryan was a tall, thin man with a balding head. He was very strict with the children but he had a good sense of humor. He believed strongly that God was in control of the world and he never missed an opportunity to share that belief with others. He often prayed in court before rendering a decision. After seeing that the horse was cared for, he came in and sat down in the living room and shared with his young family a story of God's care which would remain with Willy the rest of his life.

"It has been rumored for several days that the Regulators were on the prowl again," he told his wife Mariah while Frances and Willy listened and wide-eyed Russell cooed in his crib. "With the victories by General Sherman and General Grant they figure the war is almost over, and I guess they want to be sure all the Democrats have learned their lesson."

Silas paused for a drink of the strong Irish tea Mariah had prepared for him, and then resumed the story. "I had just set out on my trip back here to Salem and was traveling along a country road about ten miles west of here when a young boy waved at me from a

field where he was hoeing corn. At first I just waved
back, thinking he was being friendly. But when he
kept on, I realized he was trying to flag me down.
Well, I've never been one to pass up someone who
needed help, so I pulled my buggy over to the side
of the road and stopped.''

Mariah smiled when he said that. Her husband was
known all over the country for being a man you could
call on for help, and she was proud of him for it. Many
times before the war he lent a hand at harvest time
and barn raisings to the very men who now disliked
him so much and called him a "Copperhead."

'' 'Howdy, sir,' the boy said when I stopped. 'Just
wanted to warn you that some hooligans are accosting
one of our neighbors just up the road a piece. Don't
know what your politics are, but he's a Democrat and
they're some Union Regulators from up north.'

'' 'Guess there's no other road to where I'm
heading, boy,' I told him. 'But thanks for the
information anyway.'

''Well, I certainly didn't have any desire to face
a bunch of Union Regulators who were already
worked up against the Democrats, and besides that,
I was anxious to get on home. So I climbed out of
the buggy and knelt right there in the road and shared
the whole problem with God. I figured he could do
the best job of handling it anyway. Then I climbed
back up, urged the horse on and rounded the corner.
Sure enough, a group of Union hooligans had backed
a farmer up into a corner of the fence and were letting
him know just what they thought of Copperheads. As
I drove up one of them recognized me and yelled,
'Hey, it's the judge!' When he said that they all turned
to look, and I figured it was my turn to be accosted.
Instead they stepped aside kind of surly-like and let
me go right by, and in the meantime the farmer had

ducked through the fence and disappeared into his field of corn.''

His story complete, Silas Bryan stood his son up and looked him right in the face. ''Now, Willy, don't you ever forget when you get in a tough situation that the first thing to do is to pray.''

Willy Bryan got himself into several tough situations during the next few years but he didn't always remember to pray. Not long after the incident with the Union Regulators, Willy and his older sister Fannie were playing in the parlor while their father took a nap on the couch. It was a late spring day and flies were starting to invade the house.

Fannie suggested that they cover Father's head with paper to keep the flies from waking him up, and Willy was quick to go along with the scheme. After several unsuccessful attempts to get the paper to stay in place they decided to use paste. That worked great and left the flies no place to land. But when Silas Bryan woke up and found paper stuck fast to his bald head, both Fannie and Willy wished they had prayed first.

Willy's first great ambition in life was to be a Baptist preacher. His father was a Baptist and his mother was a Methodist, so he and the other children had the privilege of going to Sunday school twice every week—once with mother and once with father. At least once each year they would have each of the ministers over for dinner, and Willy decided early that talking to all those people week after week was something he would really enjoy. Mrs. Bryan got along fine with the Baptist preachers and Silas appreciated the Methodist ministers, even if he did enjoy a little humor at their expense.

The Methodist preacher, Brother Mosser, was at dinner one day when Mrs. Bryan served a roasted kid. Silas had referred to it simply as a roast when she placed it on the table, and the entire family was quite surprised when Brother Mosser began to share a strong dislike for goat's meat.

"I've eaten just about every kind of meat there is," he told them. "Chicken, duck, pheasant, beef and pork, even venison, and the only one I've never cared for is kid. There's just something about eating goat's meat I've never liked."

Fannie and Willy looked at their father, wondering what he would say, but he just nodded his head solemnly as if he were in complete agreement with the minister and went on eating.

"Now this roast," Brother Mosser went on, "I must say, Mrs. Bryan, is some of the best meat I have ever eaten."

"Perhaps you would like some more, Brother Mosser," Silas said with a twinkle in his eye.

"I certainly would," said the preacher.

"Fine," boomed Judge Bryan. "Mariah, pass the preacher some more of that roasted goat."

They all had a good laugh then, and the preacher decided that maybe he had never had the privilege before of eating kid roasted the way Mrs. Bryan fixed it.

Willy's ambition to be a Baptist preacher continued strong until one day when his father took him to a baptismal service at the church. To his surprise there was a big pool of water right in the front of the church. The minister walked right down into that pool and began to baptize people, and Willy's eyes grew bigger and bigger.

On the way home in the buggy, he was quiet for a long time, but finally blurted out the question that had bothered him all evening.

"Father, if I were to be a Baptist preacher . . .?"

"Yes, son?"

"If I were to become a Baptist preacher, would I have to go down into the water like they did tonight?"

"Of course, Willy. That's what Baptist preachers do. They show people how to accept Jesus Christ as Savior and then they baptize them to let everyone else know they have been converted."

Willy didn't say anything more all the way home, but he was thinking hard. He didn't care much for water, and the next time someone asked him what he wanted to be, he did not say "a Baptist preacher." Instead, he had decided to be a farmer.

That ambition didn't last long either because it was based on the fact that the first love of his life, an older girl by the name of Hester Williams, wanted to marry a farmer. She promised to wait for him, but instead married one of his cousins, who was already farming.

So Willy decided to become a lawyer. Whenever circuit court came to Salem and his father was sitting on the bench, Willy scampered downtown and sat for hours on the steps outside the courthouse. The voices of lawyers arguing their cases before his father was like music to his ears. Here was a job where you could talk before crowds of people every day of the week instead of just on Sunday, and you didn't have to get into a pool of water to do it! From then on his answer was always the same, "I'm going to be a lawyer."

The war may have been the greatest event that took place during Willy's childhood, but the event that was the greatest for him was the family's move out into the country when he was six. Before that he was confined to a fenced-in back yard and severely punished on the occasions when he slipped under the fence and ran off to play. After moving to the country they had a huge yard full of cedar and maple trees to climb, surrounded by more than five hundred acres of prairie. There was a fourteen-acre deer park near the house. There were animals to care for, including a Chester White boar which Willy took to the fair and had to wash constantly to keep it clean.

After they moved to the farm more children were born—Charles, Nancy and Mary. Fannie's job was to help care for the younger children. Willy, the oldest boy, helped by working in the farm during the summer. He took on the winter chores by himself, since there wasn't enough work during that time to justify hiring extra help.

During the winter Willy's first job was to light the fire in the Franklin stove which was the only heat source for the farmhouse. He got up before sunrise, threw on a cold shirt and pants, rushed downstairs over freezing wood floors and added kindling to the few coals left from the night before. Just as the fire was burning well and he was starting to warm up he had to pull on his coat and mittens and head out to the barn to feed the cows, horses and hogs. By this time his fingers were numb from the cold but he had to pull off the mittens to do the milking because he could not milk cows with mittens on. Only then was it time to go back inside where mother had breakfast waiting.

Mrs. Bryan was a cheerful, competent woman who was just as devout a believer in God as her husband. One of her strongest beliefs was in the area of getting along with other people. She did not allow the children to criticize each other, their peers, or even casual acquaintances. More than once she told them a story about a woman who always tried to speak well of others.

"Her children decided to see how far she would carry this practice," Mrs. Bryan told them, "so they agreed one day that they would come into the room where she was working and start to criticize the devil. One by one they came into the room and each one said something derogative about the devil, seeing if they could get their mother to take his part. That lasted for just a few minutes before she had enough. ''Well children,'' the mother interrupted them, looking around on each one who was sitting idle while she worked, ''if we were all as industrious as the devil is, we would all accomplish more.''

In addition to her responsibilities with the smaller children and the running of the household, Mrs. Bryan taught school for Frances, Willy, and Russell. Willy learned his lessons until he could repeat the questions and answers without a book. Then mother set him up on a walnut table and listened attentively while he declaimed them, just like the lawyers in his father's courtroom. The children enjoyed having school at home because that meant that many a day after lessons were finished they could run through the woods, or if father was home they could go hunting for squirrels or rabbits.

Willy had been given a single-barreled shotgun as soon as his parents thought it safe for him to use it. He enjoyed nothing more than helping his father mold bullets for his muzzle-loading rifle and then tramping through the woods with him, shotgun over his shoulder, and coming back with one or two squirrels.

One afternoon when his father wasn't home, Willy decided to get his shotgun out and clean it in anticipation of their next hunt. He was certain he had emptied it after returning from their last time out, but as he carried it out into the hall he bumped the trigger and the gun boomed, blowing a hole in the baseboard of the hallway.

Willy decided he would have to be much more careful with firearms, and for a while he was. Then one day while climbing through a fence, he foolishly laid his gun down with the barrel pointing right toward the place where he was scaling the fence. To his horror, as he stepped on the wooden railing it bumped the hammer of the shotgun and discharged the cap. Had the fire from the cap reached the powder, it would have meant immediate death, but for some reason the gun did not go off. Like his father, he prayed and thanked God for protecting him.

On another day Willy and a neighbor, Henry Webster, were traveling to pick up his father at the Illinois Central Railroad Station. They stopped on the way to do some snipe shooting at a pond and neglected to release the hammer when they finished. They climbed back into the buggy and began to sing, "O, you must be a lover of the Lord, or you can't go to heaven when you die." In the middle of the song, the gun, which was between them, went off and blew a hole through the back curtain of the buggy.

That was the last time Willy was ever careless with a gun. By autumn of the year he turned ten, hunting was confined to Saturdays, because that year, Willy began his formal schooling.

2
Childhood
Decisions

Willy rose early as usual to do the chores one morning in the fall of 1870, but after breakfast he did not go to the room where his mother had been teaching the children for four years.

Instead, Silas called them all into the parlor for a time of family prayer. "Today you are leaving home for the first time," Mr. Bryan said solemnly when they were all seated and listening quietly. "I thought it right and proper to read from the book of Proverbs."

Willy wasn't surprised to hear him say that. Proverbs was his father's favorite book. Almost every day during the summer when he was working around the farm his father called him a little early for lunch to sit down with the book of Proverbs, read a chapter and then talk about it.

"I will read today from chapter six," said Silas, opening the huge family Bible which was always on a table in the parlor. "My son," he began, and Willy knew the words were directed right at him. "Keep thy father's commandment, and forsake not the law of thy mother: Bind them continually upon thine heart, and tie them about thy neck.''

Willy knew exactly what ''commandments'' his father was talking about. His mother had impressed two ''laws'' upon him; ''Tell the truth'' and ''No swearing.'' His father's great hatred was reserved for gambling. Ten-year-old Willy wasn't sure exactly what gambling included, but he knew it displeased his father.

After the Scripture reading, was family prayer. This was one of the best times of the day, as far as the Bryan children were concerned. It was reassuring to hear their father pray and to know that he was on such familiar terms with God that he could just talk to Him as he talked to one of the neighbors.

''We would ask Thee,'' Silas Bryan prayed that day, ''to care for Fannie and Willy in a special way this day as they enter upon their public schooling. Keep them safe from any harm and danger and help them to always remember the lessons their mother has taught them here at home. Above all, help them to love Thee in everything they do and say. We ask this in Your gracious and almighty name. Amen.''

Then Willy and Fannie put on their jackets, picked up the brand-new book bags Mrs. Bryan had made for them, and set off on foot for the ''Log College'' at Salem, three quarters of a mile away by the Prairie Road. In this one-room school building, Mrs. Lamb sternly disciplined and taught several grades at the same time. The children feared her even before they arrived.

Younger children sat in front of the room and older ones toward the back, but all were together at recess and lunchtime. Willy made friends easily and soon knew all the fellows and girls at the school. One day at lunchtime while they were all sitting around a big

tree behind the school, some of the older boys started
"cussing." That was the word they used for swearing,
since none of their parents approved of swearing.
Some of the older girls giggled as if they thought it
was cute, but Willy remembered his mother's laws.
Stuffing his sandwich back into his lunch sack, he
stood up quietly and walked far enough away that he
couldn't hear the cussing.

A lesson on gambling was a little harder to learn.
Mr. Bryan figured that gambling was wrong whether
you lost or won, but Willy thought that maybe a sure
thing wasn't quite the same as gambling. When one
of the older boys taught him a new card trick he was
certain he had been introduced to a sure thing.

"Look at this, Willy," his friend urged. "Think
of a number and pick out five cards that have that
number on them. Then show me the cards and I'll
tell you the number you chose."

Willy obediently chose five cards and to his
amazement the friend told him the number he had
chosen in his mind.

"Wow," exclaimed Willy. "How do you do it?"

"Simple," said his friend. "See how the numbers
are arranged? If you add together the first number
on each of the five cards, you get a number from the
lists on the cards. And that's the number you chose.
Try it once."

So Willy tried it and it worked. He tried it again
and again until he was absolutely certain it would work
every time. Then his friend suggested they try it on
someone else and called over another one of the older
boys.

"Sure, I'll do it," the boy agreed, "but only if we
can have a little wager. I'll bet my knife against yours
that you can't guess the age of my mother."

Willy looked hard at the two knives sitting side by

side before agreeing. He knew his father had paid forty cents for the knife Willy owned while the other knife was just a cheap ten-center. But he didn't see how he could lose, and then he would have two knives instead of one.

"All right," he said finally. "Choose the five cards on which your mother's age appears and I'll tell you what it is."

Quickly the boy pointed out five cards, Willy added the first numbers together and proclaimed proudly, "Your mother is thirty-seven."

"Nope, sorry," the boy replied. "Guess this knife is mine now. She's thirty-five."

Willy grabbed the cards again and looked at them closely. Sure enough, thirty-five was on each of the cards, but the five numbers added up to thirty-seven. He had been tricked.

It was a hard lesson to learn but he learned it well. He now hated gambling just as much as his father did.

During the summer and fall of his twelfth year, Willy came up with a brand-new game to play with his friends from school. They organized a "Senate" in Salem, took the names of well-known Senators like Henry Clay and Daniel Webster, and debated about reconstruction and the western lands.

The reason for this game was the fact that Silas Bryan was running for the United States Congress. He had received the Democratic nomination after serving for twelve years as a circuit judge. It was an exciting time, with parades and rallies almost every week. Often Mr. Bryan took his family along, and Willy stood on the edge of the crowd bursting with excitement and pride as people cheered his father's speeches.

Willy was naturally disappointed when election day came and his father lost. But the thrill of the campaign gave him a taste for politics which he would never lose.

Besides politics and school, Will, as he was now starting to be called, spent much of his time at church. He had always attended Sunday school twice a week. In the the morning he went to the Baptist Sunday school, which was very small, and in the afternoon to the Methodist Sunday school which was somewhat larger. Most of the children from school, however, attended the Cumberland Presbyterian Church. When Will was twelve his mother joined the Baptist church with his father and that meant that he was not expected to go to the Methodist Sunday school any longer. So he started attending the Presbyterian service with his friends from school.

The superintendent of the Presbyterian Sunday school took a particular interest in the youth who came to the church each week. He made it a point to greet them by name on the street or when they came into the store he owned. But it was the Bible lessons he taught each Sunday which made the deepest impression on Will. The Bible had always been a regular part of life in the Bryan home, but now for the first time Will was beginning to realize that it contained a personal message for him.

Will and his sister Fannie had been attending the Cumberland Presbyterian Church for almost two years when a revival came. Services at the Presbyterian church were always more exciting than those in the other churches. The Presbyterians had exciting song services led by an enthusiastic fellow named Sam Chance. People from the audience were allowed to choose songs and lead in prayer and give testimonies. But the revival was even more exciting than the regular meetings.

Just one year earlier, in 1873, the great evangelist Dwight L. Moody had gone to England with his song-leader, Ira Sankey. Reports of tremendous revival sweeping across Scotland and England encouraged evangelists in America to hold revival meetings or "camp" meetings as they were often called. Instead of just the regular Sunday services, benches were set up outside and a meeting was held every night for several weeks.

The part of camp meeting most of the young people in Salem liked was the singing. They all knew the "Gospel Hymns" which had been popularized by Ira Sankey's beautiful singing. Led by Sam Chance they sang "There is a fountain filled with blood, drawn from Immanuel's veins," "Jesus, Lover of my soul," and "Rescue the perishing, care for the dying, snatch them in pity from sin and the grave." The last song, "Rescue the Perishing" had been written by the blind singer Fanny Crosby who was also the writer of many popular songs of the day.

Will enjoyed the preaching even more than the singing. The evangelist was a young man, full of energy, who preached hard. He preached against cursing and gambling and drinking. He denounced rebellious young men and frivolous, scoffing young ladies. He condemned secret societies and dime novels and the theatre as contributing to the downfall of the nation's morals. It was the most exciting preaching Will had ever heard.

But the preacher also talked about God's love which had sent His Son, Jesus Christ, to the cross. Will had heard the story of the cross since childhood, but never until now was he impressed with the fact that Jesus had died for him, to pay the penalty for his sin.

At the conclusion of every service the evangelist asked for those who desired to be converted to join him for an after-service. After only a few nights of the camp meeting, both Will and Fannie responded to that invitation. The evangelist went over again with them the importance of placing their faith in Christ as the only One who could provide salvation. Then he led in prayer as each person accepted Christ as Savior and Lord. Will and Fannie were converted. All together more than seventy of the young people of Salem were converted during the same revival.

Silas and Mariah were thrilled when they heard that Will and Fannie had accepted Christ, but they weren't as happy to know that they now wished to join the Presbyterian Church.

"I really do not wish to do something to which you would object, Father," Will told him. "But this is something I have thought about deeply and I would like to put my membership with the Presbyterians."

In spite of his disappointment that Will was not going to join the Baptists, Silas gave his permission immediately. "I want you to join where you will be most at home," he said, "and where you can do the most good. It's time you children were forming opinions of your own. I trust that all of your decisions will be as good as this one."

That summer Will faced the first test of his new faith in Christ. He and a friend named Judd Green were hired as water boys on one of the neighboring farms. To his horror, he discovered after taking the job that they would be carrying not only water but also whiskey to the men in the fields. The evangelist had preached long and hard on the evils of alcohol, and Will had decided never to drink himself, and he wanted no part in helping others to drink.

Judd, who knew about Will's conversion, offered a solution. He would carry the whiskey and Will could carry the water. And that was the way they did it the rest of the summer.

3

Off to College

Whipple Academy. The very name sent chills up and down Will's spine. The academy meant Greek and Latin and hard study, because it was a preparatory school for Illinois College. But it also meant leaving home and all his friends for Jacksonville, Illinois. The only people he knew there were the Joneses, the family of his cousin Dr. Hiram K. Jones. Dr. Jones was a professor at Illinois College and had consented to provide room and board for Will during his academy days.

Will could not remember when he decided to aim for college. He and his parents had always talked about it from the time when he was too young to remember. He would go to college, take the highest degree offered, and then go on to post-graduate work. His parents were excited about education, and he was as well. Their parting gift when he left Salem was two dictionaries, one Greek and one Latin.

Whipple Academy, as a preparatory school for Illinois College, was housed on the same campus. It shared the college's faculty as well, eight professors in all. The college had about sixty students and the academy seventy-eight. Will's first-year studies consisted primarily of translating works like Aristotle's *Rhetoric* or the Greek New Testament into English and then discussing his translation with one of the professors.

One activity on campus excited him far more than his studies.

"Will, what are you going to memorize for the oratory contest this year?" asked one of his friends, Glenn Hulett, during the spring of their first year at the academy. "I'm going to do the peroration from Daniel Webster's 'Liberty and Union' speech."

Will looked solemn. Choosing a speech for the oratory contest was his biggest decision of the year. The winner was considered by many to be the top student in the class, since oratory was the most valued of all the skills. He had joined the literary society, Sigma Pi, immediately upon entering the academy, and the speech contest was to be between them and their rivals, Phi Alpha. It was almost time to give his first big speech, and the pressure was great.

"I thought about Webster myself," he said. "But I have decided on Patrick Henry's great patriotic speech, 'Liberty or Death.' It has the sentiment I would most like to express, and you know Professor Hamilton says we have to put our hearts into what we are saying, and not just our voices."

"That's not all the professor told you," responded his friend. "He thinks you are too timid in your speaking."

"And he says I have to work on my enunciation," finished Will. "He's right about the timidity. I was so scared the first time I gave a speech in the class that I think my knees knocking together provided more applause than the audience did. But I'm working on that and the enunciation as well."

"Well, why don't we go out to the farm this afternoon and combine practice with a little rabbit hunting," invited Glenn who lived a few miles out in the country near Jacksonville. "You can give your speech to me, I can give mine to you and then we can terrorize the rabbit population."

Will practiced diligently the next several weeks, determined to put into practice everything the rhetoric professor taught him. Professor Hamilton was particularly concerned about what he called dramatic gestures. He wanted each speaker to mark his speech in the places which could be emphasized through precise movements of the hands and then use those gestures each time he spoke.

Will worked hard but when he spoke in the contest he was just as nervous as he had been in class, and he failed to place at all. Instead of being discouraged, he started to plan for the coming year. He was going to be successful in speaking, no matter what anyone said.

Helping to cushion Will's disappointment at losing the speech contest that spring was the onset of the track and field season. As soon as the frost was out of the ground, he and Glenn and Charlie Carter were out on the field practicing the running broad jump and the standing broad jump. They practiced until their legs were so sore they could hardly walk, and then they made each other keep going until the soreness went away.

"Nine feet, Will," Charlie shouted after one of Will's attempts at the standing broad jump. "You've got me beat for sure. Guess I'll have to take up the high jump. You know, Bryan, my father always told me never to speak of anyone unless I could speak well of him. Whenever I speak of you I will always say you are a good jumper.''

None of the first-year students came close to Bryan in the standing jump that year, and with diligent practice he was soon winning prizes for the academy in the broad jump.

Still it was his desire to excel in oratory. During the second year at the academy he began Latin studies. Translating Cicero was a joy because he learned how eloquence was used to help defend righteousness and punish wickedness. His parents had taught him that principle from as far back as he could remember. It was the basic principle of the book of Proverbs which, following his father's example, he was reading and studying every day.

That year Will chose a declamation called ''The Palmetto and the Pine,'' a sentimental speech which Mrs. Jones suggested. When the final standings were announced, Will Bryan had won third prize. The judges seemed to like what he said, but there were still problems with the way he said it. Dr. Jones told him it was because he ran his words together and spoke so rapidly that people couldn't understand what he was saying. He went to work on that problem, determined to overcome it at all cost. During his practices with Glenn out in the woods he even tried talking with pebbles in his mouth. That was a technique the great Greek orator Demosthenes had supposedly tried with success.

That spring Will also vied for the freshman prize in mathematics. He had enrolled in the college mathematics course and scored one hundred in geometry, so he felt he had a good chance of winning the prize. He did well on the test, but his entry in the contest was denied because he was not yet in college.

That big step came in the fall of 1877 when he enrolled as a freshman at Illinois College. Illinois had a long history of involvement in public affairs, an area which had been of interest to William ever since his father's political campaign back in 1872. One of the early presidents of the college was Edward Beecher. His sister, Harriet Beecher Stowe, wrote *Uncle Tom's Cabin*, a book which persuaded many people to be against slavery. Beecher's father, Lyman, and brother, Henry Ward, were also active in the anti-slavery movement. Under Edward Beecher's presidency, Illinois College had become known as a center for abolitionist sentiment. Abraham Lincoln's law partner William Herndon, was once a student there, but his father insisted he withdraw because he was afraid his son was becoming a "red hot abolitionist."

William continued to live with the Joneses, who had no children of their own and often took in students from the college as boarders. Many times in the evenings, the students sat in the parlor with Dr. Jones and discussed Plato, a favorite subject of his. Or they would get him to tell about the days when he knew Ralph Waldo Emerson and Bronson Alcott back in Massachusetts. Dr. Jones still took occasional trips to Concord to lecture at the Concord School of Philosophy.

Bryan was excited about being in college. There was much to learn and many opportunities to improve his speaking ability. But he was particularly glad that all the teachers at Illinois College were Christians like his mother and father. He had heard stories of young men who, under the teaching of college professors, were led away from faith to unbelief. An especially dangerous theory just coming into some of the schools in the East was evolution. It was based on the writings of Charles Darwin in a book called *The Origin of the Species*.

Evolution was a hot topic of discussion inside and outside the classroom. Dr. Henry E. Storrs, the professor of natural sciences, wanted students to think through what they believed, so he explained that there were actually several theories as to how the world began.

"Since Charles Darwin wrote his book," he told them, "people have begun to re-examine what the Bible actually says about creation. Some even believe they can reconcile the Bible account with this new theory of origins."

"But isn't that impossible?" one of Bryan's friends, Julian Wadsworth, asked.

"Let me try to explain how they do it," said the professor, "and then you can decide. One idea is that God created life in the form of a single cell and then allowed that cell to develop through the process called evolution. Another theory is that each of the Bible days of creation was actually a long period of time corresponding to the ages of the evolutionary process. A third idea, called the nebular hypothesis, says that matter and force have always existed and it was the action of force upon matter which created the universe."

After class Bryan caught up with Julian Wadsworth walking across campus. "What did you think of that today, Julian?"

"I think that all of those ideas end up in the same place. They eliminate any need for God at all."

"I don't know," William said thoughtfully. "It is not easy to explain all the differences between what scientists are saying and what I have always been taught about the Bible."

"But you don't have to explain them," said Julian. "You just have to believe the Bible."

"That's fine for you, Julian. You're going to be

a preacher. But I'm going into public life and like Dr. Storrs said, I need to know what I believe. I think I'm going to write a letter to Robert Ingersoll and ask him what he thinks about God."

"Robert Ingersoll, the agnostic?" Julian was shocked. "Isn't he the one who stands up on the platform and pulls out his watch and yells, 'God if You are really there I'll give You ten seconds to kill me'?"

"I've heard that he has done that. But he is also a great thinker. Julian, I've been taught the Bible all my life, now it's time for me to hear what those on the other side say so I can make up my own mind, once and for all."

"I suppose you are right, William. Be sure to let me know what you decide."

Bryan spent several hours writing his letter to
Robert Ingersoll. He asked specific questions about
God and the Bible and evolution, questions like the
one about the nebular hypothesis which Dr. Storrs
had mentioned in class. When the answering letter
arrived it was a great disappointment. Mr. Ingersoll
had sent a copy of one of his speeches and a form letter
that didn't answer any of his specific questions.

"Well, did Mr. Ingersoll convince you to become
an agnostic?" Julian asked him after hearing that
Bryan had received a reply.

"Not at all," said William. "I'm ready to stick with
the Bible. I think it will be just as valuable to me in
the practice of law as it will be to you in the practice
of the ministry."

"Hey, Will," Glenn shouted across campus to him
one day soon after the second term had started. "Did
you see the sign down on the Opera House? The
college declamation contest is open to the public this
year and will be held on the stage of Strawn's Opera
House. Shall we give it the old college try?"

"Sounds good to me," called back Bryan. "I'm
thinking of using President Lincoln's 'Gettysburg
Address.' I know it is rather recent but it is attaining
great popularity. What do you think Professor
Hamilton will think of that?"

"I don't know. He really prefers the dramatic pieces
to the oratorical, you know. And since he is always
one of the three judges it's probably better to
memorize something he likes."

"You're right, of course. I expect I shall take the
professor's advice, as much as I would like to do a
famous oration instead."

The professor's advice was a dramatic piece,
"Bernardo del Carpio," and this time the years of
hard work paid off. Bryan was awarded second place

in the contest and allowed to choose two books as a prize. He chose an Oxford Bible and a volume of the works of Shakespeare. Even though he didn't enter it in the contest, he worked on Henry Clay's "The Ambition of a Statesman" and gave it in front of his literary society.

By that time, Bryan's reputation as an orator was well-known on campus. The college newspaper reported on one of his speeches by saying, "Next followed the treat of the evening in the shape of an oration by W.J.Bryan. In both composition and delivery it equaled anything that has been heard in Sigma Pi for years."

Bryan was now writing his own speeches in addition to memorizing the declamations of others. In one of his essays called "Perfection," he talked about the eloquence of his favorite Roman orator Cicero. "What a power has eloquence," Bryan said. "What more enviable attainment is there than the ability to control by a stream of passionate words the thoughts of a multitude, to guide by a look the wills of your heare or to excite action by a wave of the hand." He went on to explain that Cicero had not used eloquence for the purpose of furthering his own ends, but had instead worked for justice for those who were less fortunate than he. This, Bryan felt, was the noblest use of eloquence, to speak in a court of law on behalf of those who were oppressed.

Not all of his speaking engagements were a great success, however. During the summer of 1880, Bryan agreed to give his first political speech for the Democratic presidential candidate, Winfield Scott Hancock. The speech was to be given at a farmer's picnic near Salem, and the handbill announced that there would be three speeches that day, with Bryan's being the last. When he reached the farmer's grove he found an audience of six people, the farmer, three operators of a lemonade stand and fortune wheel, and the two other speakers. After waiting an hour for the audience to arrive, they canceled the meeting and Bryan hiked back home, his speech undelivered.

Toward the end of William's second year at Illinois College, the Sigma Pi society was invited to a social gathering at the Jacksonville Female Academy. During the course of the evening Bryan was called on to give his declamation by Henry Clay on "Ambition." While he was speaking he noticed that a petite, dark-haired girl with big brown eyes was watching very closely. He couldn't remember her from previous visits to the Female Academy.

As soon as his speech was over and the applause had ceased, he made his way across the room to where she was sitting. But once there, the old shyness returned and he blurted out, not a prepared speech, but the only thing he could think of to say, "I don't recall seeing you before."

"I've just arrived," she said, smiling sweetly. "Your cousin Mrs. Jones is an old friend of my aunt. My name is Mary Baird."

What he said after that he could never remember. But it was one of his most effective speeches ever. From the Greek and Roman orators, he had learned that genuine emotion was the key to successful speaking, and that day there was no doubting the fact that his heart was in everything he said.

4

Romance, Studies and Speeches

Mary Baird was not as impressed with William Bryan as he was with her the first time they met. He saw a young lady with a quick, easy humor, graceful movement, and intelligent conversation, all of which pleased him. She saw a broad-shouldered, handsome young man who always sounded like he was giving a speech when he talked to her.

After the social gathering that evening, the girls from Jacksonville Female Academy exchanged notes.

"Did you see that fellow I was with all evening?" one of Mary's friends exclaimed. "Isn't he just the most adorable? Did you even see him, Mary? Or were you too busy talking to that William Bryan, the orator."

Mary smiled easily. "I guess I did listen to him talk for quite a while, though I wouldn't say that I did much talking to him."

"Well, I'll tell you what I think, Mary. He's just too good."

"What do you mean?"

"Well, all the fellows from the college say that he walks around as if he wore a halo. He doesn't smoke or drink or even curse. In fact, he walks away from the other fellows when they start cursing. He's just too good."

The more Mary thought about that the more she realized that it described just the type of man she was looking for. She didn't drink or smoke or curse either, and she didn't see how any of those habits made a man more desirable. So she began looking forward to the next time she would see William Bryan.

The students from Illinois College had a favorite name for Jacksonville Female Academy. They took its initials and called it the Jail For Angels instead. The principal at the academy, Mr. E.F. Bullard, did not allow any callers at the school except on very infrequent occasions, such as the night Bryan met Mary. So the fellows had to create other opportunities to catch a glimpse of their "angels."

Each afternoon the academy girls left the campus for their exercise time, a stroll around the town square. Although they were not allowed to stop and talk to any of the college students it was at least an opportunity to see each other. William began finding any number of errands to run about that time of the afternoon so he would just happen to be near the square as the girls went by.

Weeks passed, and Bryan became convinced that he was in love with Mary. The need to talk to her became so important that he climbed a tree next to her dormitory window and called to her, risking the wrath of Mr. Bullard on both of them if he was caught.

Finally they were able to make a satisfactory arrangement. Mrs. Edward Allan Tanner, wife of the Latin professor, invited William to come over to visit her family one night each week. Then she sent an invitation to the academy inviting Miss Mary Baird to visit them on the same evening. As the activity of the Tanner family swirled around them, the young couple sat in the parlor and talked, content with their long-desired opportunity to become better acquainted.

During the winter of that year, Mary's mother became sick and was brought to a Jacksonville hospital for treatment. Both Mary and William visited her regularly, and it was not too difficult to make arrangements for those visits to occur at the same time. After visiting with Mrs. Baird, William would take Mary back to the academy in a buggy borrowed from the Joneses, but often they took the long route, riding several miles into the country and back over the wintry, snow-crusted roads.

William was anxious for Mary to meet his parents as well, particularly his father. Bryan felt sure he would approve strongly of his choice, and he desired that approval very much. When Silas made a trip to Jacksonville in March of 1880, his cousin, Mrs. Jones, invited Mary to an afternoon tea, arranging the meeting through the principal, Bullard himself, so there would be no problem with the academy. Silas was anxious to "look over" the young lady who seemed to mean so much to his son.

Mary carefully chose just the right dress for this important occasion and with the help of several classmates chose accessories and arranged her hair to perfection. Then she waited anxiously.

As she watched out the window of the dormitory for the buggy that would take her to the Joneses, there was a knock on the door. A young boy handed a letter to the girl who answered it with the instruction that the note be given to Miss Baird immediately. Mary opened the letter and could hardly believe what she read. Silas Bryan had died during the night of a paralytic stroke. William and his mother were leaving the next day to take his body back to Salem for the funeral.

Silas Bryan had been fully prepared for death. He arranged for his funeral service, choosing the psalms, hymns and Scripture text which would be used. Although William and the rest of the family missed him greatly they knew of his faith in God, and that same faith sustained them through their time of loss. During the days before the funeral, the body of Judge Bryan lay in state in the county courthouse while people filed by to pay their last respects. After the church funeral, six of the leading judges and lawyers in Illinois carried his casket to the grave. William had lost his father, but he would never lose the example of honesty and integrity his father had given him.

By spring Mrs. Baird recovered enough to return to her home in Godfrey, thirty miles away, and the hospital visits and buggy rides were over. The two young people enjoyed weekly visits to the Tanner's, and they sought additional opportunities to meet as well. Eventually word of their frequent courting got back to Principal Bullard. He requested that Mr. William Bryan come to see him without delay.

"And what do you have to say for yourself, young man?" Mr. Bullard asked when William was seated in his ofice. "You are aware, are you not, that you have been seeing Miss Baird in direct violation of the academy rules?"

"But the academy gave her permission to visit the Tanners, sir," Bryan answered respectfully. "Mrs. Tanner wrote and requested it herself."

"Without informing us that you would also be a guest on those evenings, I might add. But I am far more concerned about the reports of regular and long buggy rides through the countryside."

"I must confess, sir, that you have heard correctly. But they were with the permission of Miss Baird's mother who was here in town under the care of a doctor. We did not feel that we would need the permission of the academy, having obtained Mrs. Baird's permission. However, if you feel we were wrong in that, I am prepared to accept responsibility for everything. It was my idea and my buggy, sir."

"It was definitely wrong," Mr. Bullard roared, "and an absolute breaking of our rules. Miss Baird has violated the privilege of the academy and you have acted in a manner dishonoring to the name of gentleman. You are dismissed, Mr. Bryan."

William went back to his room at the Jones's and waited anxiously for word of what would happen when the principal called Mary in to talk. He wasn't sure how she would do it, but he was sure she would try to contact him when she knew what Mr. Bullard had decided to do. Late that afternoon, Glenn Hulett came pounding on his door with a letter from Mary.

"Am going on the seven o'clock train, but it would not be safe for you to go down, would it?" she wrote.

"I'm going to Godfrey," Bryan told Glenn, tossing the note onto the table next to his school books.

"But you can't," Glenn protested. "Mr. Bullard will never allow it. You know he won't let her out of his sight until she is safely on the train."

"Then I will have to stay out of his sight," answered William and promptly set off on foot for the railroad station. Arriving just before the horse-drawn coach from the academy, Bryan purchased his ticket, climbed on the train and made his way through the passenger car and into the baggage compartment.

When Principal Bullard arrived with his ward he looked around carefully before placing her in the compartment, then watched like a hawk from the platform until the train was well out of town. Satisfied that he had done his duty, he left to return to the academy and William stepped out of the baggage car of the train and took a seat next to his sweetheart.

"Oh, William," she exclaimed. "You did come after all."

"Of course. I couldn't let them send you off alone. What did he say?"

"Well, he was really quite nice about it," Mary smiled through her tears of joy at seeing William beside her. "He didn't expel me, though he let me know that he would certainly have been right in doing so. He simply suspended me for the rest of the spring term. I can come back to school in the fall."

"In the fall? How can I possibly go that long without seeing you? Let's go straight to your parents and ask their permission to get married."

Mary laughed at the impetuous spirit of her beau. "Before you even ask my permission?" she said with a twinkle in her eye.

For the first time in his life, William Bryan was at a loss for words. "Well . . . of course . . . I thought . . . will you?"

"I wouldn't have it any other way," Mary said softly. "But I don't think it would be best to spring both my suspension and an engagement on my parents at the same time. I think you should get off the train at the next station, go back to Jacksonville and let me break the news of my suspension to my parents alone. Then, at the appropriate time you can approach them with your request."

Leaving Mary at that time was not what he wanted to do, but William could see the wisdom in what she said. Reluctantly he climbed off the train at the next station and headed back to the college.

The young couple had one opportunity to see each

other before the long summer vacation. Mrs. Jones
decided to hold a May Day party in the woods pasture
which they owned on the edge of Jacksonville and sent
an invitation to Miss Baird to come up for the day.
When Mrs. Jones and Miss Baird arrived at the field
a farmer came running out of the woods shouting a
warning to them.

"Don't go in there. There is a man in the woods
shouting and waving his hands. I think he must have
escaped from the mental asylum. He's probably
dangerous."

Knowing that William had come out to the pasture
an hour early to practice a speech, the two ladies
guessed exactly what the farmer had heard. They
enjoyed a good laugh when they told Bryan that his
speaking had caused someone to think he was an
escapee from the asylum.

During the summer of 1880 many discussions took
place around the kitchen table of the farm near Salem.
Silas Bryan had clearly spelled out in his will, that
all of his children receive a college education. William
specifically was to finish Illinois College and then
spend a year at Oxford University in England. In
order to provide for the expense, his father had
purchased thirty steers which he was fattening for sale.
However, Silas had also co-signed a debt for $15,000
as a favor to a friend, and that friend had defaulted
on his note.

The family knew that Silas would want them to pay
their debts first, even if through legal action they might
have been able to avoid paying the note for his friend.
By the time they paid the debt there was no money
left for Oxford. They finally agreed that William
would return to Jacksonville that fall to finish Illinois
College. If they could get enough money together he
would go on to law school in Chicago. If not, he would

return to the farm to run it while Russell went to college. William was perfectly willing to work in order that his brother might have the chance at a college education. However, that August Russell died, and Bryan returned to Jacksonville sorrowful over the loss of his father and brother, yet knowing that it was up to him to succeed since he was now the head of the family.

That fall the romance between Bryan and Mary continued, although Mr. Bullard restricted them to a single letter per week and no meetings outside those officially sanctioned by the academy.

For the oratorical contest that fall, William chose a speech on "Justice." He prepared what he felt was an outstanding introduction. He had heard Wendell Phillips give his famous lecture on "The Lost Arts" in Jacksonville, starting the speech with a reference to something right there in town. That gained the attention of the audience, and from there Phillips led into the topic of his speech. Bryan had noticed that the Apostle Paul did the same thing in his sermon in Athens, "As I passed by and beheld your devotions, I found an altar with this inscription, TO THE UNKNOWN GOD. Whom therefore ye ignorantly worship, him declare I unto you" (Acts 17:23). Using that idea Bryan prepared his introduction, and worked hard on the body of the speech. He won first place in the contest. Along with the win came the opportunity of representing the college at an oratorical contest to be held in Galesburg, Illinois, with schools from all over the midwest.

The competition in Galesburg was fierce and even though he received a perfect score from one of the judges, Bryan wound up in second place. The prize was fifty dollars, which he added to the money he had been saving since spring, and purchased an engagement ring for Mary, a garnet set in gold.

They agreed that Thanksgiving vacation was the proper time for him to approach her father for permission to marry her. As that time drew nearer their weekly letter spoke of little else.

"I trust you will not be frightened," Mary wrote, "though I imagine it would be a rather disagreeable task. Being a girl has a few advantages after all. If he presents the least difficulty there is a party concerned who can and will manage him."

When the big day arrived Bryan faced his future father-in-law in the parlor, armed with that which he knew best, the Proverbs.

"I have been reading," he told Mr. Baird, "where Solomon said in the book of Proverbs that 'whoso findeth a wife, findeth a good thing and obtaineth favor of the Lord.' "

Mr. Baird who had suspected he would be approached for some time and shared his daughter's sense of humor, decided to reply in kind from the Scripture. "Yes, I believe Solomon did say that," he said, trying to look solemn. "But Paul suggests that while he that marrieth doeth well, he that marrieth not doeth better."

William hadn't seen Mr. Baird very often, and wasn't sure what to think. He tried to come up with another Proverb that would answer Paul but instead remembered a bit of Bible history he thought he could use to advantage. "Don't you think Solomon would be the better authority on the subject of marriage," he asked Mary's father. "After all Paul was never married, but Solomon had seven hundred wives."

Mr. Baird laughed heartily. "You have me there. If he could have seven hundred wives and still recommend the married state, he must have been the best authority. You have my permission and Mrs.

Baird's as well. God bless you, my son.''

Mary, who had been listening outside the door, rushed in then and gave her father a big hug, showing both of her parents the ring William had purchased with his contest winnings. They were going to be married, in spite of Principal Bullard.

5
William Jennings Bryan: Attorney At Law

Bryan enjoyed his senior year in college as much as all of the previous years put together. He was engaged to be married, he was serving as chaplain of his class, and his grades were high enough that it seemed likely he would be valedictorian and deliver the commencement address. He didn't even mind coming in second in an essay contest that year because the winner was a good friend of his who William felt deserved to win.

Sam Eveland was already in his thirties when he started college. He had worked in logging camps, moving as often as was necessary to find work, and had never had a chance to receive an education. One evening he walked into a church where a revival meeting was in session, became converted, and immediately felt a call to preach. Bryan thought of the change in Sam's life every time he heard salvation spoken of as the "new birth." That was the only way to describe what had happened to Sam.

Knowing he needed schooling in spite of his age, Sam enrolled at Illinois College, where he was fourteen years older than the average age of his classmates. That fall when the Professor of Political Economy announced that everyone would write an essay on "Pauperism, Its Causes and Remedies," William knew that Sam would have a great advantage just because of his experience and background, but he did his best anyway. Sam won and Bryan got second, but he had never been happier with the outcome of a contest in all his years of school.

For his commencement address as the valedictorian of his class, Bryan chose the topic "Character."

"We launch our vessels upon the uncertain sea of life alone, yet not alone, for around us are friends who anxiously and prayerfully watch our course," he told his fellow graduates. And then, with the funerals of his father and brother fresh in his mind, he continued, "God grant that we may all so live as is meet in the better world, where parting is unknown."

Mary also gave a valedictory speech that spring upon her graduation from Jacksonville Female Academy. Even with her month of suspension she had finished with her class and achieved the highest grades of all the girls who graduated with her.

That fall the couple began the longest time of separation since they had met. Bryan and his friend Glenn moved to Chicago to begin their studies at Union College of Law, and Mary moved back home to wait until he could afford to support a family.

Chicago was as much different from Jacksonville as the latter had been from Salem. It was ugly, to Bryan's thinking. He had never seen slums before or such crowds of people. And the facilities of the college were not impressive, even though it had a reputation as the best law school in the state. It was housed in one building on Dearborn Street. There was one small lecture room, an office shared by all the faculty, a room for the secretary, and a combination coat and lounge room. The library was on the roof and had to be reached by climbing two iron ladders.

In order to save money, Glenn and William rented a room at a cheap boarding house on the South Side which provided both room and board for four dollars a week. He walked the four miles back and forth to college in order to save the five-cent transit fare and not be more of a burden on the family finances.

The courses at Union Law were much to Bryan's liking. There they studied by the case method which meant that they were assigned to read actual records of judicial decisions. Then they discussed those cases in class and were expected to remember them so they could use the same arguments those judges had used. The result was that they learned to think with great rapidity.

William's favorite cases were those which involved constitutional law. He had never given up his idea of gaining the seat in congress which his father had failed to win, and studying law as it related to politics was the most direct route to that achievement.

Bryan did not forget his church activities while living in Chicago. Although he left his church membership in the Presbyterian Church in Jacksonville, he attended church regularly and became involved in the work of the Young Men's Christian Association as well.

The topics discussed at Union were the same ones he would later face after entering political life. Students debated the prohibition of alcohol, whether women should have the right to vote, and whether or not the nation should make other countries pay a tax or tariff on items which they sold in the United States. William was in favor of prohibition, in favor of letting women vote, and against the tariffs.

His opinion on one of the biggest issues of the day was formed by his association with the man in whose office he worked, Lyman Trumbull. Trumbull was a former United States Senator who had known William's father. He was also a former associate of President Lincoln. He paid Bryan five dollars a week to sweep floors, copy documents, and make sure he was supplied with paper and ink. Since his son Henry was a student at Union, William got to know the family outside the office as well.

Lyman Trumbull was a man devoted to principle. He had broken ranks with his own Democratic party before the Civil War to oppose slavery and support Lincoln. As a Senator he drafted the Thirteenth Amendment which made the Emancipation Proclamation permanent. Now he was leading the fight in Illinois against what he felt was the greatest danger of the day, the monopolies.

"Look at how things are right here in Chicago," he told William and Henry and another friend, Adolph Talbot. "Great corporations are making a very few people lavishly rich at the expense of the common workers. These men work for hours in the factories, the packing houses and railroads. The owners of those institutions become enormously wealthy, but they make their laborers work under wretched conditions at sinfully low wages. Mark my word, there will be serious trouble ahead for this country if something is not done about this injustice."

"Let's go see for ourselves," Henry challenged the other two fellows after listening to his father. "I can't believe that conditions are really as bad as he says they are."

So one afternoon after classes the three fellows

caught a ride on the tram and headed out to Pullman, Illinois, the company town where men were building railway sleeping cars under the auspices of the Pullman Palace Car Company. George Pullman had improved the sleeping car and introduced dining cars and parlor cars to the railroads. All of these were built in Pullman with his company holding a virtual monopoly on the sleeping-car business. He had made a fortune many times over.

What the boys saw in Pullman astonished them. The town was a virtual slum, and yet the people were required to live there as a condition of employment. Boys who should have been in school were sitting on the street corners gambling for pennies instead. The obnoxious odor in the workshops was almost more than they could stand. Everything was dirty and dark, and the men were paid barely enough to provide food for their families. Then they were expected to buy that food at stores owned by the company which charged them more than stores in Chicago did for the same items. It took only one visit to convince Bryan and the others that Mr. Trumbull knew what he was talking about.

Bryan's letters to Mary were filled not only with the sentiments of romance, but also with the realities of life in Chicago. He told her of their trip to Pullman and how the railroads, and also steel and oil, were ruled by big business. He echoed the words of Mr. Trumbull in predicting that within a few years the workers would revolt against their poor working conditions and low pay unless something was done.

Mary's letters in return were bright and cheery, full of the many things she was learning from her mother in preparation for setting up a home. She admonished William to slow down and take time to eat right so he wouldn't face any health problems.

They both agreed that it would not be right for them to get married until he had a job. During the summer before his second year at Union he traveled to Troy, Missouri, where his father had once lived and then on to Kansas City, but he wasn't happy about either as a future home. Both he and Mary decided the best choice of a place to live was Jacksonville. They liked the town and they were already known, which was a great advantage for a young lawyer.

In spite of the fact that he was known in the community, Bryan's practice did not grow rapidly. After graduation from Union, he joined the law firm of Brown, Kirby and Russell, but discovered that most of the work he did was collecting debts. His first client was a saloon keeper named John Sheehan.

"I don't reckon you'll take this job," Sheehan said when he first came to see Bryan, "you being a teetotaler and all."

"Well, you're right that I don't drink myself," grinned Bryan. "Nor do I advise drinking. But I do think that those who buy liquor ought to pay for it. Sure, I'll take the job."

Within a day William knocked on the door of the saloon, calling Mr. Sheehan out into the sunshine to give him the money he had collected.

"And were they mightily upset with you for coming?" he asked. "Those folks are known for their vicious tempers."

"Not at all. In fact, as much as I hate to see it, they will probably be back to buy from you again."

Bryan was careful not to make any of the debtors from whom he collected angry. Some of them even became his clients when they saw how he could be both gentle and persistent. One stable owner agreed to pay the debt he owed if Bryan would collect some debts that other people owed him.

Other opportunities soon presented themselves to the young lawyer as well. In November, just four months after he opened his own law office, he gave his first speech to a jury in an assault case. When he wrote about it to Mary he confessed that it was somewhat frightening, "but my fright left me and I never spoke with more fluency and earnestness than I did that day."

The business was growing slowly, not fast enough to provide for the new house and other items Bryan felt he needed in order to get married. Impatient to set a date for the wedding, he arranged to borrow money against the eventual sale of his father's farm and in the spring of 1884 he and Mary chose a site for their first home. In June he walked the graduation line at Illinois College once again, this time receiving his Master's Degree.

That summer the Democratic national convention was held in Chicago. Bryan desperately wanted to attend but he knew he couldn't afford it since he was setting aside everything possible in preparation for marriage. There was a feeling nationally that this might be the year the Democrats would be able to elect their first president since the Civil War.

The people of Greenwood, Illinois, invited Bryan to deliver a patriotic Fourth of July address that summer, and after speaking, the Chairman asked him about any expenses he had coming.

"Nothing more than what it cost me to rent a buggy," said William, "not quite three dollars."

"Well, we really are glad you came," replied the Chairman. "That was the best speech I've heard in all the time we've been having these festivities here in Greenwood, and I can remember most of them. Perhaps this will cover your expenses."

Bryan looked down at the money the man thrust into his hand and recognized that it was a twenty dollar bill. He was so surprised he forgot to thank the man.

Twenty dollars was enough to cover the coveted trip to Chicago, so along with Carl Epler, the son of one of the Jacksonville judges, he attended the convention.

When they first arrived in Chicago they made the rounds of the headquarters for all the candidates, listening to the arguments in favor of each one. Then they started looking for a way to get into the convention proceedings themselves.

"Let's go over to the Illinois headquarters," Carl suggested. "There is sure to be someone there that we know."

"Good idea. Tickets can't be that scarce."

But they were. There were no tickets left at all, but Telas Merritt, a politician from Salem thought he knew of a way to get the young men in.

"There's this doorkeeper I know by the name of Joseph Mackin," he told them. "He's from Chicago, and if anyone can get you into the convention Joe Mackin can."

Sure enough, as soon as Mr. Merritt explained the situation to Joe he passed the two in as observers, and every day for the rest of the week he did the same thing. The convention nominated Grover Cleveland, who later won the presidency, the first Democrat to do so since James Buchanan, Lincoln's predecessor.

One day not long after they returned to Jacksonville, Carl came running into Bryan's office waving a newspaper. "Look at this, William. Joe Mackin, the one who let us into the convention? Well, he was just sent to the penitentiary for stuffing the ballot box at the last election."

"Isn't that something?" Bryan said as he read the article. "I guess that just goes to show us that we have met a genuine Chicago politician."

Finally, after five years of courtship and four years of being engaged, the wedding day arrived. On October 1, 1884, Miss Mary Baird became Mrs. William Jennings Bryan. The wedding was held at the Baird home in Perry with only a small group of close friends in attendance. The officiating minister was none other than Dr. Tanner, the Latin professor whose wife had encouraged them by making possible their weekly meetings in her parlor. He was now the president of Illinois College. William's younger brother Charles served as his best man.

Following the ceremony they spent a night in a hotel in Jacksonville and then traveled down to Salem for a reception arranged by Mariah Bryan and attended by more than half the town. The rest of their honeymoon was spent in St. Louis, choosing furnishings for their house, which was almost complete. When they moved into the new home in late November, Mary's parents joined them. It was not unusual at that time for parents to live with newlyweds, and since Mrs. Baird was still quite sickly, everyone agreed that those arrangements were the best.

William had promised Mary's father that he would not marry his daughter until he could be assured of at least a $500 dollar a year income. By the end of 1884 his growing practice had earned him $700, a fact he proudly shared with his new father-in-law. The next year it rose to one thousand dollars and the following year to $1500. That was a far cry from the $2.50 he had made during the entire month when he first started as a lawyer. But there was still a goal in the back of Bryan's mind which had nothing to do with making money. He wanted to run for Congress. Southern Illinois was Republican country, and Bryan was first and foremost a Democrat. Both he and Mary realized that eventually it would mean another move.

6

William Jennings Bryan: Congressman

Mary Bryan, in spite of often urging her husband to slow down and not work so hard, was a hard worker herself. Just one year after their wedding she gave birth to a daughter, Ruth. With her mother in the home to help care for the new infant, Mrs. Bryan enrolled in courses at Illinois College, joined a German conversation club, and started to read her husband's law books in order to prepare herself for taking the bar examination. She felt that becoming a lawyer herself would be one of the best ways she could help her husband in his work.

Mr. Bryan was thrilled to watch his new daughter grow and learn. Family life at the Bryans quickly fell into the pattern it would follow all of the years there were children in the home. After breakfast Bryan read from the Bible, often choosing the book of Proverbs. Then the family gathered around the piano to sing hymns with Mary accompanying them. Finally a prayer by either William or Mr. Baird would prepare them all for the work of the day to come.

In addition to his growing attorney's practice William Bryan found many ways to occupy his time. He was elected president of the YMCA and chancellor of the Knights of Pythias, a friendship organization for helping the poor and other charitable works. He taught Sunday school at the Presbyterian Church, remembering the influence which its superintendent had on him in earlier years. He spoke occasionally for the Sigma Pi literary society at the college and coached some of the student orators as they prepared for contests. He attended Dr. Jones's monthly discussion nights and helped to organize such civic events as Fourth of July celebrations.

His greatest love outside of his family, however, was politics. During those early years as a lawyer he learned politics from the ground up. Naturally sociable, he took to the streets, organizing various areas for Democrats who were running for local offices. Others, remembering his success in college oratorical contests, invited him to speak on their behalf, and soon he was traveling all across the southern part of Illinois stumping for the election of fellow Democrats.

But he would rather have been stumping the state in his own behalf. After four years there didn't seem to be any possibility of running for even a local office. The Republicans were just too strong in Illinois.

"Be patient," Mary told him. "God will lead us to make the right decision when the time comes."

During the summer of 1887 Bryan was asked to take a trip into Kansas to collect some debts which were owed to Illinois College. Hearing of the impending trip, his father-in-law suggested that he stop in Iowa to look at some property the Bairds had owned for many years. In order to do that he had to travel by train through Lincoln, Nebraska, so he wrote to his old friend from Union Law College, Adolphus Talbot, and asked to spend the weekend with him. Talbot wrote an enthusiastic letter in return, welcoming the chance to renew his acquaintance with Bryan.

Bryan liked what he saw in Lincoln. It was a frontier town, growing rapidly, and the capital of the state of Nebraska. It seemed to the young lawyer to be a place of limitless opportunity, a sentiment which Talbot encouraged.

"You ought to move out here," he told his friend. "Why, the city is just crying for lawyers, not like back there in Illinois where they are a dime a dozen."

"But I'm just getting to the place where my practice is growing strong," Bryan protested. "And I have a family to consider."

"They'll love it here. Lincoln is a great place to live. And as to your practice, well, why not become a partner with me. I have more than enough work to do and need to have a partner anyway. I can't think of anyone I would rather work with than William Jennings Bryan."

Bryan took a walk and thought about the possibility of a move to Nebraska. Stopping in at one of the newspaper offices, he began to talk with the editor, and within a few minutes was offered the chance to write a weekly column answering legal questions submitted by readers. It seemed that Lincoln really was hungry for legal advice. By the time he left for Iowa he had decided that Lincoln was the place to be. All that remained was to convince Mary.

To his surprise she was completely ready to move. "You know Jacksonville," she said, "and you have seen Lincoln. If you think that a change is for the best, I am willing to go."

On October 1, 1887, their third wedding
anniversary, Bryan left for Lincoln, promising to build
a house and send for his family as soon as it was
complete. The house in Jacksonville was put up for
sale and Mr. Baird advanced money for the new house
to the young couple, with the arrangement that he
would be repaid when the Jacksonville house sold.

Talbot and Bryan opened their new offices in the
First National Bank Building of Lincoln, and William
moved a cot into one of the rooms for a place to sleep
until he could have a house built. By June of the
following year the new house was complete, and
Mary, Ruth, and the Bairds came to join him in
Nebraska.

The house on D Street was a two-story Victorian structure with a glistening white exterior. A large porch circled all the way around the front and the building was crowned with an observation tower from which they could see much of the sprawling frontier city.

Lincoln had grown from a village of fifty people to a population of over 40,000 in just twenty years. Most of the growth was a result of being the hub of railroad activity west of the Mississippi River. Through Lincoln flowed silver from Colorado, wheat and beef cattle from Wyoming, and copper from Montana, all heading east. In the other direction the trains carried thousands of settlers to claim free lands being offered under the Homestead Act.

Dolph Talbot served as an attorney for the Union Pacific Railroad, a position which bothered Bryan greatly. The Union Pacific and the Burlington had been granted millions of acres of land on either side of their right-of-way when they laid their track through Nebraska. It was some of the best acreage in the state, and controlling that land made the railroad companies the most powerful political force in the state. The railroad bosses had some of the state legislators on their payroll, and they controlled others by contributing large amounts of money to their campaigns. Bryan knew that when he ran for office he didn't want to be controlled in any way by big businessmen.

He and his partner had a simple way of sharing their business. At the end of each month the one who had made the most would divide in half the extra amount he had made and share it with the other. However, Bryan insisted that the money Dolph made from the railroad not be included in their totals. He wanted nothing to do with what he considered tainted railroad money.

Apart from that small disagreement the two men had a very successful partnership. Dolph was a Republican, which made the two of them acceptable to customers on both sides of the political fence. He was a very religious man, a staunch Methodist and firm believer in the same Biblical views held by Bryan. When they were working on a case, Talbot developed the line of argument while Bryan debated the other side, taking the place of their opposing attorney. That way, when they arrived in court they had already anticipated the arguments the other side would use and were prepared to answer them.

As their legal practice grew, so did their acquaintance with influential people throughout the state. Bryan joined the Knights of Pythias, of which he had been the chancellor back in Jacksonville, and also the Chamber of Commerce, the Rotary Club, the Elks, Odd Fellows, Masons, the Moose, the Royal Highlanders and the Modern Woodmen. He and Mary moved their church membership to the First Presbyterian Church of Lincoln and very soon he was teaching Sunday school again. He became an industrious member of the YMCA and often gave lectures to the young men on the subject of temperance.

All this activity was, in Bryan's mind, a preparation for his entrance into politics. He was completely aware of the fact that a man who wanted to run for office had to know as many people as possible. He also knew that Nebraska, like Illinois, was a state of staunch Republicans. He had brought letters of introduction from prominent Illinois Democrats but he didn't really need them. There were so few Democrats in Lincoln that anyone who wanted to join the party was welcomed with open arms. They immediately began to give Bryan invitations to speak at their meetings, and what they heard excited them. Here was a

Democrat who knew what he was talking about, and knew how to say it, as well.

The big need in Nebraska, Bryan thought, was for someone who would speak for the farmers. Leaders of both the Republicans and his own party were controlled by the railroads. And the railroads were the worst enemy of the farmers. They controlled the cost of sending produce to market, so that by the time farmers paid the railroads they had almost no profit left for themselves. With those small profits farmers had to buy goods which were high priced because of tariffs the government charged on items imported from other countries.

So Bryans's first speeches were against the tariff, a position he had learned from Mr. Trumbull while he was in law school. He compared the tariff to a cow, which he said was fed by the Western farmers, but milked by the Eastern industrialists. That was something Nebraska farmers could understand, and they cheered him wildly.

Returning from one of the meetings where the crowd had been most enthusiastic, Bryan woke Mary from sleep.

"Mary, I had a strange experience. Last night I found that I had power over the audience. I could move them as I chose. I have more than usual power as a speaker."

Then they both knelt by the bed while he prayed and asked God to help him use this power of speaking in a wise fashion, on behalf of the people, just as Solomon had prayed for wisdom many years before.

One year after moving to Lincoln, Bryan was elected to the state convention and intived to speak. Although he was addressing state delegates, he did not hesitate to give a recipe for national victory. He urged his party to take up the cause of the farmer, the laborer, the common man who had no one to represent him. Let them oppose the tariff which impoverished the common man and fight for the rights of farmers against big businesses which were oppressing them. The speech brought him statewide recognition. J. Sterling Morton, the leading Democrat in Nebraska, insisted that Bryan accompany him to the national convention in St. Louis. There Bryan spent his time meeting leaders of the national party while the delegates nominated Grover Cleveland for a second term in the White House.

Bryan was also offered an opportunity to run for lieutenant governor of Nebraska, which he declined. He was willing to help others run for state office, but he was interested in running only for the Congress of the United States.

All through that summer and fall he stumped the state on behalf of Morton's candidacy for the United States House of Representatives. His speeches were a great success and were reported as such in newspapers all over the state. In spite of his speaking, however, Morton lost in the state and Cleveland lost the presidency to Benjamin Harrison. It was a strange election, in that Cleveland won a majority of the popular vote but Harrison won in the electoral college. From that time on, Bryan was in favor of popular election of the president and of abolishing the electoral college.

After the excitement of the election, it was good to settle down to his law practice in Lincoln once again. Mary, having completed her law studies, passed the bar examination and became a lawyer herself. And in 1889 a son whom they named William joined the growing family.

On Bryan's birthdays, his favorite gifts were books on political science. He read extensively on the tariff and how it hurt agricultural states such as Nebraska. He became more and more convinced that if the Democrats were ever to win an election it would have to be by forming an alliance with the farmers of the state. Most of the farmers were Republicans, but they opposed their own party on the subjects of the tariff and the railroad monopolies.

In a special election for State Supreme Court justice that year the Republicans, as usual, swept the state. But Bryan noticed that Douglas County went for the Democrat.

"Look at this," he told Mary. "Douglas County is one of the largest in our own First Congressional District. If a man could carry Douglas County and do well here in Lincoln he could be elected to Congress."

"Even a Democrat?"

"Even a Democrat. It's time this string of Republican victories came to an end. I predict that in the next election a Democrat will win the congressional seat from Douglas County."

Mary smiled as she looked up from feeding little William. "And who do you think that man ought to be?" she asked, knowing full well the answer.

7

Friend of the Farmers

Life was not good for the farmers of Nebraska in 1890. Three years of drought had destroyed their crops, and hard winters had killed their cattle. Many people lost their farms and land because they were unable to make the high payments owed to the bank. Where a few years before the wagons were heading west, they were now abandoning farms and moving back to the East. In just one year eighteen thousand prairie schooners crossed the Missouri River at Omaha heading east and leaving the farms behind. On the sides of their covered wagons people hung signs which read, *"In God we trusted, In Nebraska we busted."*

Many farmers who remained blamed the railroads for much of their trouble. They figured that half of their profit on crops was eaten up by freight charges, and Nebraska farmers were paying more to transport their grain by train than farmers across the river in Iowa. When they tried to get the state government to regulate the high rates, they got nowhere. The railroad owners were so rich that they were able to pay off lawmakers with free railroad passes and even direct bribes.

The farmers also blamed the large industrial trusts for raising the prices of machinery, fertilizer, and clothes higher and higher, while the prices the farmer got for his corn and wheat dropped lower and lower. The third villain was the tariff. Tariffs had been written to protect the big businesses from foreign competition, but nothing protected the farmer from competing grain imports. If Canada or Mexico wanted to sell their corn at a lower price than the American farmer, they could do it.

"Nebraska grows three great crops," wrote one angry editor of a farm country paper, "corn, freight rates and interest. Corn is produced by the farmer who farms the land. The other two are produced by men behind bank counters who farm the farmers."

To Nebraska farmers the answer to their problem seemed quite simple. People weren't able to buy their crops because of a shortage of money. If they had enough money they could buy corn at a price which would be fair to the farmers. Silver was produced in abundance by mines in the Rocky Mountains. If that silver could be changed into coins and put into circulation, the money problem would be solved. The idea was called "free coinage of silver."

In 1890 both the Democratic and Republican parties in Nebraska were controlled by the trusts and railroads who favored the tariffs and a gold standard rather than free coinage of silver. So the farmers decided to form a new political party called the People's Independent Party. They didn't really think they had enough votes to win the election, but they felt that perhaps they could influence the person who did win to help them with some of their problems.

When the Democrats met to nominate a candidate

for Congress in the spring of 1890, there was no one who wanted to run against Republican William J. Connell. Connell was popular, had the railroads behind him, and seemed a certain winner over anyone the Democrats could run against him.

Because of all the speaking Bryan had done across the state in the previous election, some Democrats asked if he would be interested in running against Connell, and to their surprise he agreed to try. So the party nominated William J. Bryan for the House of Representatives seat in the first congressional district, the very seat he had predicted to Mary would be won by a Democrat in the next election.

Once he had the Democratic nomination sewed up, Bryan began working to be nominated by the new People's Independent Party, as well. He agreed with them on the tariff, he opposed the railroads and the trusts, and he was willing to work for the free coinage of silver, although he didn't know much about that idea. He began to read everything he could on free silver.

Many farmers heard Bryan speak and were in favor of nominating him, but the convention nominated, instead, Charles Van Wyck, who had previously served in Washington as senator. Bryan was disappointed but set out to win as many votes from farmers as he could, even without the additional party nomination.

Bryan wrote the platform which the Democrats adopted in their convention, and it included all the issues of the day. It called for the abolishment of trusts, for popular election of Senators, for free coinage of silver, and it opposed the McKinley Tariff. Bryan's speech to the convention was a powerful challenge for the common men of the state to join him in the fight against big business. "I shall go forth to the conflict

as David went to meet the giant of the Philistines,"
he told the crowd, "not relying upon my own strength,
but trusting to the righteousness of my cause."

Immediately after the convention Bryan set off on
a whirlwind campaign trail, determined to visit every
part of the large congressional district he hoped to
represent. When he and the Democratic candidate for
governor, James Boyd, came to town it was like the
Fourth of July and the county fair all rolled into one.

As large wagons carrying Bryan and Boyd rumbled
into a village they were met by the local Boyd and
Bryan club. The crowd carried large banners
proclaiming the arrival of "The next governor and
representative of the great state of Nebraska." A band
from the local high school led a parade, banners came
next, followed by as many people with torches as the
local club could round up. Then came the wagons with
Boyd and Bryan standing in the back waving to people
who watched from the sidewalks and windows in town.
When they arrived at the town hall or city park there
was a picnic dinner for everyone, followed by speeches
from the candidates.

James Boyd always spoke first because he knew he
was not as exciting a speaker as Bryan. When he
finished telling the people why they should vote for
him as governor, Bryan climbed up on the back of
the wagon so everyone could see him and began his
speech.

The topics were almost always the same, trusts,
tariffs and money. But the way Bryan talked about
those topics made even the children in the audience
feel that they could understand them. "When you buy
one dollar's worth of starch," he told the farmer's
wives, "you pay sixty cents for the starch and forty
cents for the trusts and the tariff."

"The great masses of our people are interested not

in getting their hands into other people's pockets,''
he told workers in the cities, "but in keeping the hands
of other people out of their pockets.''

To farmers who were frustrated that no politicians
would listen to them, he said, "When the poor and
weak cry out for relief, they too often hear no answer
while the rich, the strong, the powerful are given an
attentive ear.''

Everywhere he went crowds swarmed to hear him
speak and often cried out for more when he was
finished. Newspapers began to write about how close
the election was going to be between Bryan and
Connell. But everyone realized that the new People's
Party was going to take votes from the Democrats
instead of from the Republicans, and that almost
assured a victory for Connell.

Hoping to remove some of that advantage which
Connell held, Bryan challenged him to a series of
debates. Connell, who apparently hadn't heard of
William's success as a debater, agreed, and eleven
debates were held in as many cities and towns. Many
who could remember thirty years ago, compared these
debates to the Lincoln-Douglas debates which had
taken place then in Illinois.

Three thousand people crowded into Bohanan's
Hall in Lincoln for the first debate, and they were not
disappointed. Bryan attacked his opponent with vivid
illustrations of the effect of the tariff, just as he had
done on the stump. "Class legislation is dangerous
and deadly,'' he shouted. "It takes from those least
able to lose and gives to those who are least in need.''
Time and again applause swept through the hall as
he spoke.

It was obvious to everyone who heard them that
Bryan was a much better debater than Connell.
Newspapers which supported the Republican

candidate began to attack Bryan viciously, afraid that he might actually pull off an upset victory. "Mr. Bryan went to church, leaving his mouth in the backyard practicing on a new tariff speech," one newspaper gibed. Another one described his speeches as being "as effervescent as a bottle of soda pop."

Then one month before the election, Charles Van Wyck, the People's Party candidate, withdrew from the race. The party quickly nominated someone else, but it was too late for him to do much campaigning. Reports began to come in from all across the district that independents were switching their support to Bryan.

By election day the unthinkable had been accomplished. Bryan beat Connell by over six thousand votes, to become only the second Democrat in all of Nebraska's history to represent the First District in the Congress of the United States. At the same time James Boyd was elected governor of the state.

During the months before the new session of Congress started, Bryan continued to study the money situation as it related to the coinage of silver. He became convinced that this really was at the bottom of all the money problems in the United States. If the government would accept both gold and silver as money currencies, that would mean a great deal more money available, and it would solve the financial problems of the farmers.

In November Bryan left for Washington, D.C., to take his place in Congress and look for housing. After several lonely months he returned in February to get his family, which now included a little girl named Grace, who was born during his absence. Mary's father went with them as well. Her mother had passed away in Lincoln.

Being in Congress was exciting for the young Bryan, now only thirty years old. Eighteen generals of the Civil War were congressmen, as well as others whose names Bryan had heard many times and was now able to meet.

Through his friendship with Congressman William Springer, Bryan was appointed to the Ways and Means Committee, the most powerful committee in the House of Representatives. That was something almost unheard of for a congressman in his first year as a member of the House.

William and Mary threw themselves completely into the work of representing Nebraska in the House of Representatives. Mrs. Bryan walked to the Library of Congress almost every day to do research for her husband. Then she listened as he worked on his speeches, carefully choosing the exact words and phrasing them in a way which would have the most impact on his audience.

On Sundays the family attended church in the morning and spent the afternoon calling on friends on Capitol Hill. Often the group of friends would share a time of hymn singing and light refreshments before returning to their homes.

The attention of the nation was focused on this hard-working first-term congressman when he gave his first speech on a favorite subject, the tariff. Most speeches on the subject were guaranteed to put listeners to sleep, but not Bryan's.

A bill had been introduced to reduce the tariff charged on imported wool. On March 16, 1892, Bryan rose to speak in favor of the bill. Mary, who was sitting in the gallery, noticed that soon after he began to speak the seats near her were all filled. Soon people were standing in the back of the balcony, as word spread of the exciting speech the young westerner Bryan was giving on the tariff.

"The tariff is a monster which transfers money from one man's pocket to another man's pocket," Bryan charged. "A slave is a slave because all of the proceeds from his toil are taken by somebody else without his consent. So we are all slaves of the tariff."

As the speech progressed Senators stopped in from across the hall and the House chambers became as crowded as anyone could remember since the great debates of Webster, Clay, and Calhoun just before the Civil War. "The manufacturers gather around a banquet board to celebrate 'home industries' at ten dollars a plate, when within a stone's throw of their banquet hall are people to whom a ten-cent meal would be a luxury," said Bryan, and then concluded, "We desire that the laws of the country shall not be made, as they have been, to enable some men to get rich while many get poor."

For more than three hours he debated with the pro-tariff forces, defeating them on their own ground and proving his point to the satisfaction of Democrats and Republicans alike. Representatives from both sides of the aisle rushed to shake his hand after the speech, moved by the force of his oratory. "This is the first time I ever left my seat to congratulate a member," called out Congressman Kilgore of Texas, "but it is the first time I ever had such great cause to break the record."

Newspapers across the nation reported the speech with descriptions such as "an oratorical firecracker" and "wonderfully brilliant." One hundred thousand copies of the speech were sold. With one speech William Bryan became known across the nation as one of the leaders in Congress.

In 1892 Bryan was up for re-election in Nebraska, and in spite of his national reputation his chances for election seemed even more slim than two years before.

The national Democratic party nominated Grover Cleveland, who was opposed to free silver. The state party nominated J. Sterling Morton for governor, who was also opposed to free silver. Although they re-nominated Bryan, the party let him know that free silver was not going to be part of their platform that year.

The People's Party, now known as the Populists, once again refused him their nomination, so the race was going to be fought three ways instead of two. The Republican nominee was Allen W. Field, a judge from Bryan's home town, Lincoln, and the speaker of the Nebraska state legislature.

Field and Bryan had eleven formal debates but also found themselves speaking from the same platform at county fairs. Because the tariff was the main issue of the election, Field brought along a suitcase full of items such as bolts of cloth. He held these up and explained that they were made in Nebraska and were protected from competition by the McKinley Tariff.

Then Bryan stood up and opened his suitcase. Laying a set of butcher knives on the table in front of him he began to speak quite casually. "I am something of a traveling man myself," he said. "On a recent trip to Mexico I bought this American made cutlery for half of what it costs here in Nebraska. The manufacturer, thanks to the tariff, can charge us here in Nebraska double prices and then dump the rest on the foreign market and still make a twenty-five per cent profit."

Then he turned to the farmers in the audience. "What did you get for your wheat last year?" he called.

"Eighty-five cents," came back the reply.

"What did you get this year?" he asked again.

"Fifty cents," they called back.

"Great is protection," Bryan said mockingly with his hand in the air, "and yet my opponent insists that you should buy his goods in order to keep some of his eastern friends warm and make them comfortable."

On the day of the election the race between Fields and Bryan was too close to call. For four days votes kept coming in from various precincts giving first Bryan and then Field a slight majority. It wasn't until every vote was counted that Bryan was declared re-elected by a margin of only one hundred and forty votes. Big businessmen from the East had sent the Republicans more than $20,000 to help defeat him. Big name politicians like William McKinley had come to campaign on behalf of his opponent. Even parts of his own party had opposed him, but in spite of all that, he won the election. The "golden-tongued orator of the West" was on his way back to Washington.

8

Golden-Tongued Orator in Washington

In the election of 1892 which returned William Jennings Bryan to the House of Representatives, the nation also elected a Democrat president, Grover Cleveland. It was Cleveland's second term, although in between his two terms Benjamin Harrison had been president for four years. Even though they were both Democrats, Cleveland and Bryan were not in agreement, particularly on the question of silver. Cleveland wanted the nation to remain on the gold standard and stop coining silver. Bryan wanted the nation to use both gold and silver as money.

Even before President Cleveland was inaugurated, his followers tried to get Congress to repeal the Sherman Act, which required the government to buy silver and make it into coins. Opposed by Bryan and by Richard Bland, one of the leaders of the silver forces, the attempt to repeal the Sherman Act failed.

Less than two months after Cleveland became president, the nation was hit by a financial crisis called the Panic of 1893. Major railroads such as the Union Pacific, and the Sante Fe and the Reading, faced bankruptcy. Banks failed in every state, and the people who had money in those banks lost everything. Soon four million people were without work, and many of them were living on the streets, especially in factory towns where the industries owned the homes of the workers. Farmers in the South and West were not able to sell their crops because no one had the money to buy them.

There were many reasons given for the panic, but Bryan and his followers believed there was one major reason. They believed that rich men in New York and London had caused the panic to try to put pressure on Congress to maintain the gold standard.

More and more invitations were coming for Bryan to speak on the financial situation the country was facing. During the summer of 1893 he traveled across the West and South speaking to such groups as the Trans-Mississippi Congress; the Young Men's Democratic League of Atlanta, Georgia; and the Bimetallic State Convention in Topeka, Kansas. He even had invitations in the North from such places as Ann Arbor, Michigan, where he addressed the University of Michigan Democratic Club. Everywhere his message was the same: America needed to act for itself and declare both silver and gold to be legal tender.

"One hundred and seventeen years ago the Liberty Bell gave notice to a waiting and expectant people that independence had been declared," he told approving crowds of people. "There may be doubting, trembling ones among us now, but, sirs, I do not overestimate it when I say that out of twelve million voters, more than ten million are waiting, anxiously waiting, for the signal which shall announce the financial independence of the United States.''

Everywhere he went people cheered, and some began to mention his name as a possible candidate for president in 1896. No one took that suggestion very seriously except Bryan himself. He felt that the issue of silver was the main issue facing the American public. If Cleveland was not willing to support free silver, then the Democrats needed to nominate someone who would.

President Cleveland, true to his promise as a candidate, called a special session of Congress in one more attempt to repeal the hated Sherman Act. Immediately Bryan left his speech-making circuit and traveled to Washington to lead the silver forces in battle once again. Writing back to Lincoln where Mary was staying, he told her how important he thought the vote was. ''I believe our prosperity depends upon its right solution and I pray that I may be the instrument in the hands of Providence of doing some good for my country,'' he wrote.

It was announced not long after the debate began that Bryan would speak on August 6. Knowing that this was likely to be the key address of the entire session, every member of Congress was in his place. The gallery was crowded and people stood along the walls and jammed the hallways.

Bryan had prepared a written text and it lay on his desk before him, but when he began to speak it was without the use of the notes. He stood tall and strong, a handsome figure dressed simply and yet smartly in western boots, a black suit, white shirt and black string tie.

In a short introduction Bryan praised President Cleveland for his honesty, courage, and sincerity, but

then reminded his listeners that mothers in India possessed the same three qualities when throwing their infants into the Ganges River as a sacrifice to their gods. He compared the effect the gold standard would have on the dollar to "lending a Nebraska neighbor a hog weighing 100 pounds and the next spring demanding in return a hog weighing 200 pounds."

As Bryan spoke he described a choice he felt his party had to make. Would they choose to support the "imperious and compassionless corporate interests and moneyed institutions" or would they work on behalf of "the masses, work-worn and dust-begrimed, suffering from the inequitable distribution of wealth, unable to purchase necessities?"

This speech was just as popular as the earlier one on the tariff, but this time Bryan did not win the vote which followed. The House repealed the Sherman Act in accord with President Cleveland's wishes. In spite of losing the vote, Bryan's popularity across the country increased. He and Mary received more than a hundred letters a day, more invitations to speak than he could possibly fulfill, and over 150,000 requests for the speech.

The repeal of the Sherman Act did not solve the nation's money problems as President Cleveland had hoped. Instead they grew worse as people rushed to banks with their silver certificates and demanded to be given gold in exchange. The depression grew worse as more and more people lost their jobs.

Bryan offered several ideas to Congress during that session which seemed radical at the time, but they were later adopted into law. He proposed that banking reserves be spread throughout the country instead of just being kept in the large Eastern banks. That idea later became a part of the Federal Reserve System. He also advocated a national income tax of two percent on any annual income over $4,000.00. He believed that the system of taxation in place at that time took seventy percent of the income of poor people away from them while collecting only three percent of the income of the rich. He felt that a national income tax would correct that inequity.

The income tax was passed by both the House and the Senate, only to be declared unconstitutional by the Supreme Court. It would be many years before income tax was recognized as the most equitable way of levying taxes on the nation.

Cleveland, while rejecting Bryan's ideas, continued to be plagued by trouble in the country he was trying to lead to prosperity. In May of 1894, workers at the

Pullman Company in Chicago called a strike against their company. Pullman company leaders refused to discuss anything with the workers, and soon Eugene V. Debs, who was head of the powerful American Railway Union, took up the cause of the workers. He called a general strike against the railroads, and throughout the North, rail lines were paralyzed as men refused to work. Violence broke out and President Cleveland realized something had to be done.

Since railroads carried mail, Cleveland obtained an injunction from a judge which said the mail could not be obstructed, and then sent the army to break up the strike. The effect in the West was similar to the reaction of the colonies when the British fired on citizens of Boston just before the Revolutionary War. They were outraged that the President had sent troops.

Faced with the prospect of another close election, Bryan decided not to run for the House of Representatives in 1894, but instead allowed his name to be entered for the United States Senate, a post which was appointed by the state legislature at that time. He also became editor of the Omaha World-Herald, the largest Democratic newspaper in Nebraska. In the election that fall he received 75 percent of the popular vote, but the Republicans controlled the State Legislature and they sent off his opponent to Washington as senator. Bryan had another reason to support direct election of senators and the president.

With his two terms in the House at an end and no immediate prospect of serving in the Senate, Bryan set about building up his law practice, editing the World-Herald, and fulfilling the many requests for speaking which came across his desk. Everywhere he went his coming was celebrated with fireworks, red, white and blue bunting, and brass bands. Men sold hats with the silver slogan ''16 to 1'' printed on them. 16 to 1 was the ratio at which silver backers thought silver should be valued when compared to gold. Games were organized to entertain the children while their parents listened to a rousing speech endorsing the return to a silver coinage.

The nation continued to suffer from the results of the Panic of 1893. A small group of unemployed people called Coxey's Army walked to Washington, D.C., to give Congress a visible symbol of what it meant to be without work. When they got there they were arrested for trespassing on the Capitol grounds and some of them were even clubbed.

One of Bryan's most important speaking engagements was in Springfield, Illinois, just one month before the Democratic Convention of 1896. It was called by the governor of Illinois, John Altgeld, and Bryan was the principal speaker. President Cleveland, feeling that the Springfield conference was a direct attack on him, arranged for a meeting of his own in Chicago during that same time.

Just before the national convention, Bryan lost two of the people who were closest to him. Lyman Trumbull's funeral was held on June 27 and three days later Mariah Bryan, his mother, was buried in Salem, Illinois.

Bryan went to the Democratic National Convention in Chicago as a delegate from Nebraska and not as a candidate for president. The leading candidates were Richard Bland of Missouri and Horace Boies of Iowa. Both had strong support but neither one had enough votes to assure him a first ballot victory. Newspapers that remembered to mention Bryan, listed him as seventh among the possible candidates.

The convention was held in the Coliseum, a huge building with row upon row of seats for the 906 delegates, plus enormous galleries for guests. Most of the men who rose to speak were not heard beyond the rows occupied by delegates. But the strong voice of Bryan could be heard to the farthest reaches of the galleries where his wife Mary sat watching the entire proceeding.

Although he was a member of the Resolutions Committee and wrote several of the planks, he was not the Chairman and therefore did not expect to participate in the debate over the resolutions. To his surprise, the Chairman of the committee, Senator Jones of Arkansas, asked him to take charge of the debate on the platform. This was exactly the opportunity Bryan had been waiting for, and immediately he began "polishing" the speech on silver which he had delivered so many times over the course of the last several years.

When word of Bryan's impending speech spread throughout the convention hall, groups of delegates from North Carolina, Iowa, and Kansas announced openly that they were prepared to vote for him for president. But newspapers were still predicting a win for Bland on the third ballot.

The morning of July 9, 1896, found the auditorium crowded long before the scheduled opening at 10:00 A.M. Bands played "Dixie" and "My Maryland" and other popular songs while people waited for the proceedings to get under way. Finally, after the usual opening ceremonies, the debate on the platform was announced by the reading of the various planks recommended by the Resolutions Committee. As one man after another rose to speak for or against the resolutions the crowd became more and more restless, for most of the men's voices did not carry up into the galleries.

The time came for the final speech. William Bryan

sprang from his seat and strode onto the platform as applause and cheering spread across the floor and up into the galleries. For several minutes Bryan stood completely still with one hand resting lightly on the lectern and the other stretched out over the crowd appealing for silence. But the cheering only grew louder as people climbed up on their chairs to see over the top of those who were standing.

When silence finally was restored, Bryan began to speak in a voice which he did not raise at all and yet was able to project to those in the farthest seats. "The humblest citizen in all the land when clad in the armor of a righteous cause, is stronger than all the hosts of error," he proclaimed. "I come to speak to you in defense of a cause as holy as the cause of liberty—the cause of humanity."

With every sentence he spoke, the crowd became more and more excited. Every time he paused to breathe they rose and shouted their approval and then sat down in absolute silence as he moved on to his next strongly-worded idea. He began to list all the business interests of the nation which he said the Easterners had defined too narrowly. As he mentioned the farmers, the merchants, the attorneys, and the miners, large groups of men representing those occupations rose and cheered, each trying to outdo the display of the previous group.

Finally he arrived at his stirring conclusion, the words which would echo around the world as the battle cry of the silver movement. "Having behind us the producing masses of this nation," he declared, "we will answer their demands for a gold standard by saying to them: You shall not press down upon the brow of labor this crown of thorns, you shall not crucify mankind on a cross of gold."

As he stepped back to leave the platform the entire

auditorium was silent, transfixed as it were by the vivid image he had just described. He was almost down the steps and onto the floor when the room exploded with sound. Delegates grabbed the nearest items they could find and waved them in the air. People waved banners, handkerchiefs, hats, newspapers, canes and even chairs. Delegates fought their way through the crowd to shake Bryan's hand. A man from Kentucky started down the main aisle carrying his state banner and soon delegates from Alabama, Nebraska, and other states joined him until hundreds of the delegates were marching around and around the chairs cheering and shouting "Bryan! Bryan! Bryan!" For twenty-five minutes the demonstration continued for the man who was not even supposed to have a chance of receiving the nomination for president. To all but the most loyal Bland supporters it was evident that the young Bryan was a force to be reckoned with when the time came for nominating a candidate for president of the United States.

9

The Great Commoner

The enthusiasm set off by William Jennings Bryan's "Cross of Gold" speech spread through the city of Chicago and to other parts of the nation. A reporter called Canton, Ohio, to tell the Republican candidate, William McKinley, that his opponent would very possibly be William Bryan, but McKinley refused to believe him. Governor Altgeld of Illinois predicted that by the morning after the speech the temporary support for Bryan's candidacy would be "as dead as a doornail."

It wasn't until 8:30 the following evening that the chairman of the convention began calling for nominations. Senator Vest rose to place the name of Richard Bland in nomination. His followers tried to show some of the enthusiasm the Bryan men had displayed the night before, but Vest's speech just wasn't that exciting. Following him a Georgia delegate Judge Henry Lewis came to the platform, supposedly to make a seconding speech for Bland. Instead he announced that he wished to present "a sterling Democrat, come to lead the Israelites to battle, William Jennings Bryan."

The convention exploded once again at the mere mention of Bryan's name and for fifteen minutes the aisles were crowded with marchers while the chairman tried to restore order. Finally at an hour well past midnight all the nominations had been made and the convention adjourned until 10:00 the next morning before starting the balloting. Bland and Boies and Altgeld were afraid that if they started the balloting that night there would be no stopping the stampede to Bryan. They wanted the rest of the night to talk to people and convince them he was not the man for the job.

Instead, rumors spread through the hotel lobbies across Chicago reporting that the southern states and even Illinois were considering switching from Bland to Bryan.

When the first ballot was taken, Bland was leading, but not by enough to win the nomination. Bryan, who had been listed in seventh place by the newspapers, was second. A large number of delegates abstained, either because they were gold men or were waiting to see which way the vote went.

On the second and third ballots both Bland and Bryan gained votes, but by the end of the fourth roll call Bryan had moved into first place in the balloting. When that announcement was made, another great demonstration began with marchers circling the Coliseum waving huge banners and pictures of Bryan over their heads. One after another the banners of the states which were now voting for Bryan joined the procession. An Illinois delegate, who had been Bryan's classmate at Illinois College, grabbed their banner and joined the parade even though their delegates were still pledged to Bland.

Finally the chairman restored order and began the fifth roll call vote on nominations. Alabama voted for

Bryan. Colorado switched their votes from another candidate to Bryan. Kansas dropped Bland and voted for Bryan. Then it came time for the Illinois vote. Governor Altgeld stood in the middle of his delegation, which had left the hall earlier in the day for a conference. "Illinois," he announced, "casts its forty-eight votes for William Jennings Bryan of Nebraska."

Immediately the state of Ohio followed their example, and then from all over the hall came calls from state leaders who wanted to switch their votes to Bryan. Even Missouri withdrew its nomination of Richard Bland and cast thirty-four votes for "The gifted and glorious son of Nebraska."

Mary was sitting in the gallery, watching the proceedings with pride. Just thirty-six years old, her husband was the youngest man ever to be nominated for the presidency of the United States.

Bryan, who was waiting in his rooms at the Clifton Hotel, hurried down to the barber to get a shave when the word arrived that he had been nominated. The barber was so excited that he could hardly handle the razor.

Soon newspaper reporters arrived and then friends and well-wishers, and within the next few hours he shook hands with several thousand people. Even when he lay down for a short nap, the doors were left open so crowds pushing through the hallway could catch a glimpse of their hero.

On Saturday as the Bryan party packed their bags and prepared to head back to Lincoln, a representative from one of the large railroad lines showed up at the Clifton.

"Mr. Bryan," he said. "As a candidate for president of the United States it is only fitting that you return to Nebraska in style. We would like to offer

you a private Pullman car for your return to Lincoln,
for which there would be no charge.''

Bryan was flabbergasted. All his political life the
railroads had opposed him, and now that he was a
nominee for president, they were offering him free
passage in a private Pullman car, the most luxurious
railroad car made.

''Mr. Bryan, you should not accept this offer,''
spoke up a reporter friend by the name of Willis
Abbot. ''You are the Great Commoner, the people's
candidate, and it would not do to accept favors from
the great railroad corporations.''

''You are absolutely right, Willis,'' said Bryan,
turning to the railroad representative as he spoke.
''Thank you for your offer, but I will travel back to
Nebraska in the same fashion I came to Chicago, as
a common man.''

When Abbot reported the story in his newspaper
he used the same words, ''Great Commoner,'' to
describe Bryan. Soon that title gained recognition
across the nation. William Jennings Bryan was the
Great Commoner, the people's candidate for
president.

The new Populist Party met for their convention
in St. Louis later that summer and made Bryan their
candidate for president as well. But the gold wing of
the Democratic Party held a separate convention and
nominated Senator John Palmer of Illinois for
president.

Bryan's campaign strategy was simple, travel to as
many places and speak to as many people as possible
before the election. William McKinley's strategy was
just the opposite. He planned to remain at home in
Canton, Ohio, and allow the people to come to him.
When asked about specific questions like the silver
issue, he gave answers which were unspecific, designed

to please everybody. His campaign manager, Mark Hanna, raised and spent somewhere between ten and sixteen million dollars sending out 250 million pamphlets about McKinley. The Bryan campaign, on the other hand, spent about $300,000. The Republicans received large gifts of support from Standard Oil, J.P. Morgan, the railroad companies and the Chicago meat-packers. The Democrats received most of their support in small gifts from individuals.

The campaign began with Bryan's acceptance speech at Madison Square Garden in New York City. From there he set off across the country traveling 18,000 miles by train, visiting 26 states in more than 250 cities and speaking to over five million people. In one twenty-four hour period he gave thirty speeches. The total number of speeches delivered between the convention and the election totaled more than three thousand. Traveling through the night to arrive at a scheduled speaking place, he often rose from his sleep and stepped to the platform to give an impromptu speech to crowds who had gathered at the station simply to see his campaign train.

Mark Hanna asked McKinley followers to display an American flag to show their support for the Republican candidate. Bryan responded by asking people to fly flags as a symbol of patriotism rather than party, but to many people throughout the campaign, the flag became a symbol of McKinleyism.

As Bryan traveled around the country and McKinley sat on his front porch, it seemed as if the people were overwhelmingly in favor of the Great Commoner. In Asheville, North Carolina, they met him on horseback and led him into town. His route through Raleigh was lighted with burning tar barrels. All through the South and the West he was greeted by excited, cheering crowds.

Then came the time for a campaign swing up into New York and New England. Here the gold forces were concentrating their efforts to defeat him and the crowds were more hostile. He spoke in front of one factory which had a huge sign hanging over the door which read, "This factory will be closed on the morning after the election if Bryan is elected. If McKinley is elected, employment will go on as usual." The manufacturers were threatening their employees with the loss of their jobs if they voted for Bryan. At Yale University a group of boys brought a brass band into the hall which played constantly while he was trying to speak. "I have been used to talking to young men who earn their own living," Bryan called to them, "not those who desire to distribute wealth which somebody else created."

Even with the opposition of big business bosses, however, people in the East cheered Bryan almost as enthusiastically as those in the West and South. Mark Hanna appealed to the business interests for more money and even suggested that McKinley go out and give some speeches of his own. But McKinley wouldn't hear of it, he wasn't about to make the same mistake other politicians had made and start debating with William Bryan.

By October, a month before the election, a projection by the New York *Herald* gave Bryan more than enough electoral votes to win. The Commoner moved back across the nation to spend his last three weeks in the upper Mississippi states of Iowa, Minnesota, Wisconsin and the Dakotas, as well as Illinois, Indiana, Michigan and Ohio. Mark Hanna sent out an urgent call to McKinley people to "unfurl your flags, show your colors, and vote for the protection of your family." Because of a crop failure in India, the price of wheat rose dramatically during

those weeks, something Bryan had predicted would
not happen until after his election. New discoveries
of gold in South Africa and Australia convinced some
people that perhaps silver was not necessary after all.
With each of these new events Mark Hanna sent out
another pamphlet so that by the time November
arrived he had sent an average of eighteen political
items to every person who voted that fall.

On election day the Bryans were back in Lincoln.
After their usual time of Scripture reading and prayer
in the morning they voted in the fire engine house,
escorted to the polls and back by a local group called
the Bryan Home Guards. Then they waited for reports
of the election returns to come in to their library where
two telegraph companies had installed lines in order
to receive the special bulletins. By 11:00 P.M. that
evening it was obvious that Bryan had lost the election.
He had won 48 percent of the popular vote to 51
percent for McKinley and had actually received one
million more votes than Cleveland had received in his
successful run for the presidency four years before.

Mrs. Henry Cabot Lodge, a Republican, summed
up the Bryan run for the presidency in a letter to the
British Ambassador. "Alone, penniless, without
backing, without money, with scarce a paper, without
speakers," she described Bryan to the ambassador,
"that man fought such a fight that even those in the
East can call him a Crusader, an inspired fanatic—a
prophet."

10

Onward to the Next Presidential Campaign

Even though the battle had been lost, the war was not over and millions of Americans still looked to the Great Commoner as their leader. William and Mary took the first several weeks after the election gathering material and writing a book about the campaign. It was called *The First Battle*, and it sold 200,000 copies the first nine months it was in print. Income from the book made it possible for Bryan to leave his law practice in the hands of Adolphus Talbot and concentrate his energies on the next presidential campaign to come in 1900.

The house on D Street in Lincoln was home not only to Bryan, Mary, and their three children, but also to Mary's father. Dan Bride, who began working for Bryan as an aide when he was in Washington, lived with the Bryans too. After the hectic agenda of the presidential campaign, it was a relief for all of them to return to a regular schedule. They ate their meals

together around the big table in the dining room. The
family gathered in the parlor once each day for Bible
reading, hymn singing, and prayer. Even when he
was out on the road with speaking engagements,
Bryan set aside a time each morning for his private
meditation on the Scripture, as close as possible to
the time his family would be praying back in Lincoln.

The Bryans spent most of those days studying and
responding to the many letters they continued to
receive. They had a large two-sided desk in the center
of their study so that William and Mary could work
together. She continued to be his research assistant
and secretary just as she had been during his two years
in Congress.

For three years Bryan traveled around the nation
lecturing on the subject of free silver. In the mid-term
elections of 1897 the populist and silver candidates
won in many states, and it began to look as if nothing
could keep him from both the nomination and the
presidency in 1900.

Although he still felt that the money issue would
be the dominant question in the election of 1900,
another great problem faced the nation during the final
years of the nineteenth century. In 1895, a revolution
broke in Cuba as the people tried to free themselves
from Spanish rule. There was a great deal of sympathy
for the cause of the Cubans in the United States,
causing many congressmen to urge President
McKinley to send troops to aid the Cubans. Bryan,
however, urged caution. He felt that it was best to
support the President's effort to avoid war.

That issue was settled on February 15, 1898, when
the United States battleship *Maine* was blown up in
the harbor at Havana, Cuba, and 250 sailors lost their
lives. The pressure on President McKinley to declare
war on Spain became too great to resist, with Assistant

Secretary of the Navy Theodore Roosevelt leading the call for war. McKinley was still undecided. In private Roosevelt complained that the President had "no more backbone than a chocolate eclair."

On April 21st Congress declared that a state of war existed with Spain. Roosevelt resigned from office so he could recruit men for a cavalry regiment which became known as the Rough Riders. Bryan wrote to President McKinley and offered his services "at your command during the war with Spain and assure you of my willingness to perform to the best of my ability."

With the approval of Governor Holcomb of Nebraska, Bryan organized the Third Nebraska Regiment which promptly chose him as their Colonel. Although he had been opposed to the war right up until the day Congress declared a state of war to exist, he felt it was his duty to obey his government. "This war must not be a war of conquest," he declared, "but the nation must take a higher road." He felt that any nations freed from Spain during the war should not become possessions of the United States, but should immediately be granted their independence. He had been against imperialism ever since the days at Union Law College when they discussed it in the home of Lyman Trumbull.

Fifteen thousand people gathered in Omaha to see the Third Regiment leave for Florida where they were to be stationed. A fireworks display was capped with a spectacular explosion which painted the words "Welcome Third Regiment" in the air and then followed it with a hugh portrait in fire of Colonel Bryan.

Four days after the Third Regiment arrived in Florida, Spain sued for peace. Although Bryan's troops remained in encampment for five months, the war was essentially over. They never left United States soil.

On the other side of the world a naval squadron led by Commodore George Dewey sailed into Manila harbor in the Philippines, destroyed the Spanish fleet anchored there, and claimed the Philippine Islands for the United States. Now the question of imperialism was extended not only to Cuba but to the Philippines as well. Henry Cabot Lodge expressed the view of the expansionists when he wrote to Theodore Roosevelt that "Republican conventions are all declaring that where the flag goes up it must never come down."

On December 10 the peace treaty with Spain was signed in Paris. It called for independence for Cuba but not for the Philippines. Accepting his honorable discharge from military service, Bryan rushed back into the political arena, this time with a new battle to fight.

"Our people defended Cuba against foreign arms," he told his eager audiences, "now they must defend themselves and their country against a foreign idea— the colonial idea of the European nations." He felt that for the United States to set up a colonial arrangement in the Philippines was to violate the spirit of the Declaration of Independence which had sparked the revolt of the English colonies and resulted in the War for Independence.

Although Bryan was the first public leader to come out against imperialism and the annexation of the Philippines, he was soon joined by other men including former President Grover Cleveland. It became obvious to everyone that imperalism had joined the silver issue as one of the most important questions which would decide the election of 1900.

But Bryan put a third burning question before the people as he resumed his lecturing travels in 1899. That was the question of the "trusts," those great combinations of companies which had attained a monopoly over many of the country's largest industries. The first of these was the Standard Oil Company, founded in 1872 by John D. Rockefeller. It controlled 95 percent of the giant petroleum industry. Others were the American Sugar Refining Company and International Harvester, who by shutting down their smaller competitors could pay lower prices for raw materials and charge higher prices for their finished products.

Bryan was outspoken in his opposition to trusts. "There can be no good monopoly in private hands," he told his crowds, "until the Almighty sends us angels to preside over the monopoly." With these three issues providing material for his speeches, nothing could stop the march of William Jennings Bryan toward his second Democratic nomination for president. No other candidates emerged to challenge him.

As an announced candidate for the nomination, Bryan followed tradition and did not attend the Democratic National Convention in Kansas City, Missouri. Delegations from every state came to the convention pledged to support Bryan, and he was nominated on the first ballot.

The Republicans also re-nominated their candidate from 1896, President William McKinley. Since the vice-president had died in office, they had to find a new running mate for the president. Their choice was the young hero of the Spanish-American War, Theodore Roosevelt.

The nomination of Roosevelt pushed the issue of imperialism even more to the forefront of the campaign. He was an energetic speaker, strongly committed to expansion, urging the nation to acquire possessions overseas. Bryan did not recognize how proud the nation was of their defeat of the Spanish military power in Cuba and the Philippines, nor did he realize how many people were opposed to giving the islands their independence. Roosevelt, as a military hero, succeeded in making Bryan's opposition to the war look unpatriotic, even though he had volunteered and served throughout the course of the military action.

The fact that Bryan also insisted that the Democratic platform call for a 16 to 1 price comparison between silver and gold, hurt his re-election efforts. Commercial prices for both metals had changed and were at approximately 22 to 1 in 1900. But Bryan felt that a change in the popular slogan "16 to 1" would not be understood by the common people. So they stayed with the old slogan even though it was outdated.

President McKinley adopted as his campaign slogan the "Full Dinner Pail." His followers said that it symbolized the difference between the depression years under Democratic President Grover Cleveland and the years of prosperity the nation had enjoyed under Republican President McKinley. Once again Mark Hanna portrayed McKinley as the greater patriot by suggesting that Bryan wanted to lower the American flag from where it waved over the American dead. Again the Republicans received massive contributions from big business and outspent the Bryan campaign ten to one. This time, though, Hanna had another weapon. Teddy Roosevelt didn't stay on the front porch. He took to the road and gave more speeches than William Jennings Bryan.

In spite of the tremendous odds against him, Bryan threw himself into the task of campaigning with the same intensity he had brought to the election of 1896. He crossed and recrossed the country, giving powerful speeches and convincing those who were willing to listen that this was indeed the year when the voice of the common people would be heard. His contagious optimism, boundless energy and unbelievable endurance helped him to keep up a schedule which would have completely worn out four other men. Bryan introduced a new method of campaigning when he recited portions of his acceptance speech for phonograph records which could be played on Thomas Edison's new invention. In that way people who didn't hear his speeches in person could listen to them in the comfort of their own homes.

Mark Hanna, running McKinley's campaign once again, convinced factory owners and bankers that Bryan was "just as dangerous as he had been four years before." Soon factory owners were announcing to their workers that if Bryan won, their jobs would be gone. Bankers promised to give loans to people only on the condition that McKinley was re-elected.

Once again Bryan and his friends gathered in Lincoln to await the outcome of the election and once again it was clear by midnight that he had been defeated a second time. The results were almost identical to 1896; McKinley gained only one percent more of the popular vote than he had in the previous election. In thinking back on the campaign, Bryan attributed his defeat to "the war, better times and Republican money."

His second defeat would have discouraged a lesser man. But his belief in God sustained Bryan during the days following the election. He was spurred on by the conviction that he was doing what God wanted him to do. Years before, someone had commented to his father, Judge Bryan, that even though he prayed before making any decision, the Supreme Court reversed several of those decisions which the judge felt God had led him to make.

"The Supreme Court is wrong," was the judge's

ready answer. Bryan did not blame the people for his defeat, but like his father he believed that the nation was wrong. In spite of his loss he determined to continue his work and remain in political life.

11

The Chautauqua Circuit and the Editorial Pen

Just a few months after the start of his second term in office, President McKinley was assassinated at the Pan-American Exposition in Buffalo, New York. As he was shaking hands in a great crowd of people, a man with a revolver concealed under a handkerchief stepped forward as if to shake with him. Instead he fired two bullets at close range. On September 14, 1901, President McKinley died and Theodore Roosevelt took his place in office.

The death of President McKinley grieved Bryan greatly. ''The grief of personal friends and close political associates may be more poignant, but their sympathy is not more sincere than that extended by political opponents,'' he said in a public statement. Even though he had disagreed with the president and sought to replace him through the ballot box, he condemned those who tried to overthrow governments with violence. ''Anarchy can be neither excused nor tolerated here,'' he said.

With Theodore Roosevelt in office, Bryan saw a greater danger of the nation becoming imperialistic. He prepared a speech called "A Conquering Nation" and returned to the lecture circuit. "We must not give in to the bloody and brutal gospel of imperialism," he told his listeners, "where the Ten Commandments and the Sermon on the Mount are discarded and the yellow-back novel is substituted." No other political leader had such a large and loyal national following, and even though he had suffered two defeats for the highest office in the land, faithful Bryanites filled lecture halls to hear their hero everywhere he went.

Another reason Bryan was able to keep up such a schedule of speaking even though he was not in a political campaign was because of the Chautauqua circuits. Chautauqua began as the Camp Assembly for Bible Study under the leadership of two ministers who ran a camp on Lake Chautauqua, New York. They brought in speakers and developed an entire summer schedule which became very popular with students and others who came to the camp. Soon other assembly grounds began to imitate Chautauqua, and independent managers began to arrange the schedules of the speakers. In that way the Chautauqua circuit was started. A speaker who was popular at Lake Chautauqua would be scheduled into the other assembly grounds as well. Soon more than ten thousand towns were holding annual Chautauqua assemblies, and the most popular speakers were in constant demand.

William Jennings Bryan was one of the most popular speakers in the entire Chautauqua system of lecturers, which included military heroes, great explorers, politicians, distinguished foreigners, and temperance leaders. Musicians and musical groups also traveled the Chautauqua circuit.

Although he was sometimes asked to speak about silver or bring his lecture on "A Conquering Nation," the most requests from Chautauqua audiences were for a lecture he called "The Prince of Peace." It was basically a sermon, expressing in vivid language Mr. Bryan's belief that only the return of Jesus Christ would bring a lasting peace to the world.

Bryan took a very friendly, homey approach with his audiences so that each one felt he was talking just to him. He talked about familiar objects like watermelons and explained how one small watermelon seed that "took off its coat and went to work" could produce a forty pound melon, "two hundred thousand times its own weight." That seed would decorate the melon it produced with a green cover, put inside that cover a layer of white and within the white a core of red and a scattering of seeds, each of them capable of producing another forty-pound melon. Then he would make his point. "What architect drew the plan for the melon?" he asked. "Where does the little seed get its tremendous power? Until you can explain a watermelon, do not be too sure that you can set limits to the power of the Almighty or say just what He can do or how He would do it." Finally, after that strong appeal he would step back and smile as he said, "I cannot explain the watermelon, but I eat it and enjoy it."

The "Prince of Peace" lecture was reprinted many times, and people in his audience often had read it, but they still thrilled to hear him tell about a visit to Egypt where he saw some grains of wheat which had been in an Egyptian tomb for three thousand years. "There is in the grain of wheat an invisible something which has the power to discard the body that we see, and from earth and air fashion a new body so much like the old one that we cannot tell the one from the other.'' He paused while the thought of a three-thousand-year-old grain of wheat coming back to life gripped the minds of his listeners, and then continued. ''If this invisible germ of life in the grain of wheat can thus pass unimpaired through three thousand resurrections, I shall not doubt that my soul has power to clothe itself with a body suited to its new existence when this earthly frame has crumbled into dust.''

Another means Bryan had of keeping his views before the public was by publishing a weekly paper call *The Commoner*. Started just after the election of 1900, it was an immediate success with 17,000 subscribers even before the first edition was printed. Subscriptions and newsstand sales for the first issue amounted to more than 50,000 copies.

The Commoner was a family paper. In addition to the editorials written by Bryan and the reprints of his speeches it included a home department with useful hints on sewing and cooking. A ''Query Box'' printed letters received from readers which were answered by Mr. Bryan. There were also recipes for everything from strawberry Bavarian cream to gooseberry jam.

Charles Bryan, William's younger brother, managed *The Commoner*, as well as doing some of the writing. Another popular writer for the paper was Will Maupin who contributed a column of jokes, poetry, and wise sayings called ''Whether Common or Not.'' His poetry was often directed against the same social evils that Bryan opposed in his speeches.

> Mary had a little lamb
> Its fleece was thin and sickly!
> She vainly tried a tariff pill
> To make it come in thickly.
> The wool she got from her pet lamb
> By Dingley law protected

> She sold the trust, but at a price
> Much lower'n she expected.

Maupin also invented imaginary speeches to show what was taking place in Washington. These were really nothing more than jokes which poked fun at political life in the capital. "Hello, Boomerleigh," he wrote. "I thought you were holding down a seat at the Senate in Washington?" "Nope," came the answer. "Had a streak of bad luck. Just as I got my legislators rounded up for a final vote my bank failed."

Although it cost him dearly in potential income, Bryan refused to advertise liquor, tobacco, or anything manufactured by the trusts. But even without the advertiser's money the paper prospered. Within a year Charles had built the circulation up to more than 140,000.

The nation enjoyed great financial prosperity during the years following the turn of the century, but at the same time more people were becoming aware of the need for social reform. They became concerned about the evils of alcohol, or "booze" as it was commonly called, the horrible conditions of the city slums, the plight of the Negro population, the exploitation of children as laborers, and the fact that women were still not allowed to vote. Even President Roosevelt recognized the growing power of the great trusts like Standard Oil and campaigned to curb that power, eventually becoming known as the "trust-buster."

All these causes found their way into the pages of *The Commoner*. "Educational advantages should be open to both races," Bryan wrote in an article on tax appropriations for Negro schools, "and both should be encouraged to secure all the mental discipline possible." "The world," he wrote in another column, "needs the brain of woman as well as the brain of man, and even more does it need the conscience of woman."

The role of government in these areas, Bryan taught, was to protect the rights of people. "When I tell you that the first and most important object of government is not money-making or the extension of commerce or even the care of property, but rather the protection of human rights," he said in a speech at Madison Square Garden in 1904, "I am not asserting an original proposition, I am simply giving expression to a fundamental truth."

Mr. Bryan's views of social justice and equality for all people were accepted by his children as well. When their oldest daughter Ruth finished two years at the University of Nebraska, she accepted a job at Jane Addams' Hull House. Hull House was a neighborhood center in Chicago that provided everything from a day nursery for children to college courses for immigrants. It gave Ruth a chance to put into practice the Christian principles she had learned at home from her parents. Jane Addams, in addition to running Hull House, was working for many of the same reforms as Bryan—an eight-hour working day for women, child-labor laws, housing reform, and a separate system of juvenile courts.

As the election of 1904 came closer it appeared to many that the Democrats would once again turn to Bryan. The only other name commonly mentioned was former President Grover Cleveland. When the convention began in St. Louis, Bryan was there not as a candidate but as the Chairman of the Nebraska delegation. He was not committed to any candidate but was opposed to Cleveland and Judge Alton B. Parker of New York, who was being pushed by Easterners in the party.

In spite of a tremendous speech delivered to the convention at 4:30 one morning by Bryan, they nominated Alton Parker on the second ballot. It seemed as if Bryan had lost influence in the Democratic party, but before a vice-president could be selected a telegram arrived from Parker in New York informing the convention that he believed in the gold standard and would support it instead of silver. Even though it was too late to change their nomination, many Democrats went home with the realization that Bryan had been right to oppose Parker. In the election that fall he was soundly defeated by Teddy Roosevelt.

Immediately after the November election and Roosevelt's impressive electoral victory, people began to encourage Bryan to make another run for the presidency in 1908. Even though he approved of President Roosevelt's trust-busting and his efforts to give the Interstate Commerce Commission power to regulate railroad rates, he still disagreed with him on imperialism and other important issues. "I believe in speaking well of any policy that is good, regardless of which party is supporting it." he told reporters after a visit to the White House. "I have often been accused of being a Populist merely because I have given my support to some things advocated by that party. I suppose I shall now be accused of being a Republican because I agree with President Roosevelt on some things."

Bryan was particularly lavish in his praise when the President negotiated the end of the Russo-Japanese War. He wrote a public letter in *The Commoner* hailing Roosevelt as a "peacemaker" and concluding with the idea that the President must realize "how the peaceful victory thus achieved by you outshines your military exploits." He went on to encourage him to undertake one of Bryan's favorite causes, an agreement between nations to arbitrate their disagreements instead of going to war to settle them.

The fact that President Roosevelt was doing many of the things which Bryan had advocated through the years did not escape the press. In one interview with Bryan a reporter asked, "Is is true that President Roosevelt caught you in swimming and stole your clothes?"

Mr. Bryan laughed, "He didn't get all my clothes and I doubt whether what he did get fit him very well."

It was widely rumored that Secretary of War, William Howard Taft, would be the choice of the Republicans to replace Roosevelt and carry on his programs when his second term was over. Roosevelt had promised on the night of his victory in 1904 not to run for a third term in office. Before he decided whether or not to run against Taft in 1908, Bryan and his family left on a tour around the world which would last for an entire year.

12

Popular Abroad
and at Home

All the Bryan family took the trip around the world except Ruth, who was working with Jane Addams in Chicago. For Mr. Bryan it was a combination trip for work as well as sight-seeing. The newspapers owned by William Randolph Hearst invited him to write a series of articles about the travels.

The family's first stop was Hawaii where they were greeted with a large reception at the Royal Hawaiian Hotel. They were taken surf riding in native canoes, and shown the sights of the islands.

Crossing from there to Japan they arrived just after the conclusion of the Russo-Japanese War, at a time when relations between the United States and Japan were at their best. Mr. and Mrs. Bryan were invited to a banquet in honor of Admiral Togo who had won great victories over the Russian Navy during the course of the war. Taking their seats at the table of honor, the Bryans immediately turned over the empty wine glasses which were set in front of them to show the waiters that they would not be wanting any wine.

They both had been non-drinkers all their lives and they were not about to begin drinking alcohol just because they were half-way around the world and it was considered the proper thing to do.

After they all ate heartily of the banquet feast, various individuals began offering congratulatory toasts in honor of their host, Admiral Togo. As each toast was offered the guests raised their champagne glasses and drank in recognition of his great exploits. Bryan also raised his glass and drank, but he was drinking water and not champagne.

The first several times this happened the Admiral said nothing, but finally he called the English interpreter over to his side. "Why is the great American Mr. Bryan not willing to drink a toast to me in champagne like all of my other guests?" he demanded.

The interpreter in turn relayed the question to Mr. Bryan. This was a very serious matter in the eyes of the Japanese and could easily cause hurt feelings and even an international incident between the two countries. But Mr. Bryan was ready for the question. Smiling at his host he told the interpreter what to tell Admiral Togo. "Admiral Togo won his great victories on water, so I drink to him in water," he said. "When he wins a great victory on champagne, then I will drink to him in champagne."

The interpreter moved back to the Admiral and repeated Bryan's words. When he came to the part about winning a great victory on champagne the Admiral smiled back at Mr. Bryan. He was delighted with the Commoner's sense of humor, and from that time on the Bryan's visit to Japan was a great success. He was even granted an interview with the Emperor. But his happiest experiences were the visits he made to homes of the people of Japan. They weren't always sure exactly who he was (one letter he received was addressed to "My Lord, His Grace the Duke"), but they welcomed him, and he concluded that the people of Japan "entertained nothing but good will toward our nation."

When the Bryan family arrived in the Philippines they found it progressing rapidly in education and standards of living under American rule. They thought that the military government of General Leonard Wood was doing a much better job ruling the Philippines than the British were doing in India, but it was still Mr. Bryan's opinion that the Philippines should be granted their independence as soon as possible.

In the spring of 1906 they arrived in the Holy Land.

For several enjoyable weeks they visited places like
Jerusalem, Bethlehem, and the Sea of Galilee which
were familiar to them from their Bible reading. From
there they went to Europe, stopping in St. Petersburg,
Russia, to visit the Duma, the most representative
body ever allowed to assemble in Russia under the
rule of the Czar. The governments of various countries
interested Bryan more than the sights. They witnessed
the coronation of King Haakon VII in Norway, had
an audience with King Edward in England, and
met with the Prime Minister, Sir Henry
Campbell-Bannerman.

In July, the Peace Congress of the Interparliamen-
tary Union met in London with William Jennings
Bryan as the featured speaker. Delegates from around
the world who desired peace were not disappointed
by the Commoner. After almost a year without
making any speeches, he was ready to deliver one of
his best. His voice rang out through the Royal Gallery
of the House of Lords, as the audience listened with
rapt attention. He proposed "the formation of an
International Commission of Inquiry or Mediation"
to settle disputes before nations went to war. In a
dramatic conclusion to his speech he pointed to a
painting on the death of Admiral Nelson which hung
on the wall and proclaimed, "There is as much
inspiration in a noble life as in a noble death."

Finally returning to the United States, Mary and
her husband discovered to their delight that the year
abroad had strengthened Bryan's support among the
American people. The general feeling everywhere they
went was that his third nomination for President of
the United States was inevitable.

A committee of friends from Nebraska arranged for
a huge "Welcome Home" reception in New York
City. When the Bryans' steamer moved into New

York Harbor, the whistles of factories and hundreds of ships blew in unison. Mayors, governors, senators, and congressmen lined the dock waiting for their arrival. Supporters from Nebraska hauled out a huge lasso and "roped" their candidate to show their support for his nomination. From the docks the reception moved to Madison Square Garden where Bryan was to present his first speech in over a year on American soil.

Mary encouraged him not to read his speech, feeling that he was at his best when he spoke extemporaneously from notes, but he was afraid that the hostile newspapers would misinterpret what he said if he didn't read from a prepared text. As a result, the speech didn't produce the excitement that came from most of his speaking and the newspapers misinterpreted what he said anyway. Though he dealt with a great variety of topics during the one-hour speech they quoted only some remarks he made suggesting that the federal government operate some interstate railroad lines to prevent a monopoly. The hostile press did their best to make him look like a Socialist although he had specifically stated that he did not favor government ownership of all railroads.

William Howard Taft was Teddy Roosevelt's chosen and handpicked successor. He had never run for public office but had served as judge in Ohio, as U.S. Solicitor General, as a Circuit Court Judge, Governor-general of the Philippines, and as Roosevelt's Secretary of War. He weighed over 300 pounds and was about as different physically from the athletic Roosevelt as night was from day. The Republican party was ready to accept him as their candidate simply because he was the choice of President Roosevelt.

After settling his family in their new home in

Lincoln, called Fairview, Bryan set out on the Chautauqua circuit and the political campaign trail once again. He developed a new speech called "The Moral Awakening" which had a religious theme suitable for Chautauqua but which also took Rockefeller, Roosevelt, and the trusts to task.

The years began to take their toll on Mr. Bryan's youthful looks. He lost most of his hair. His waistline bulged from what was once an athletic figure. His cheeks became puffy. But his voice did not lose its strength or fervor. He could still move an audience to tears or applause with his oratory. In churches, YMCA's, schools, colleges, city parks, opera houses, and Chautauqua tents across the country he fervently championed the virtues of godliness and politics.

A difference between this lecture tour and previous ones was that now more and more of the traveling was by automobile instead of train. Roads were often no more than deeply rutted mud holes, and it was unusual to drive from one town to another without at least one flat tire. But the convenience of setting his own schedule instead of depending on the schedule set by the railroads outweighed the disadvantages.

During the intervals between his travels Bryan returned to Nebraska to enjoy his growing family. Ruth had two children of her own, their first grandchildren. She was becoming quite well-known in her own right, having authored a play produced in New York and serving as president of the Women's Democratic Club of Denver. Since she was a lecturer in the extension service of the University of Nebraska, she was able to visit Lincoln quite often. William, Jr., was enrolled in Culver Military Academy where he showed absolutely no aptitude for public speaking. Grace was seventeen and a student at Hollins Institute near Roanoke, Virginia. She loved music, fiction, and horses.

Mary and W.J. joined the Farmer's Club because the Country Club had a bar. During the winter months the Farmer's Club often met at a home, shared a pot-luck dinner, which always included chicken and a wide variety of pies, and then sang around the piano. Inevitably someone requested the hymn "I'll Go Where You Want Me To Go" because they all knew it was Mr. Bryan's favorite song.

As the election year of 1908 arrived, word came that more and more states were instructing their delegates to vote for Bryan. Some, particularly in the East, continued to oppose making him the Democratic candidate for the third time, but these people were silenced by the great majority who felt that this was the year for a Democratic victory led by the Great Commoner himself.

As various delegations traveled to Denver for the Democratic National Convention, they stopped to pay their respects to the Bryans in Lincoln. When the delegations arrived in Denver, they were met at the depot by a band and escorted to their hotels. Twenty thousand Denverites acted as a walking information bureau. They roamed the streets wearing buttons which said, "I live in Denver. Ask me." Hanging high above the convention hall were portraits of Thomas Jefferson, the father of the party, and Grover Cleveland, the last Democrat to be elected President, who had just died.

This convention belonged to Bryan from start to finish. On the first day in a speech by Senator Gore of Oklahoma the mere mention of Bryan's name sparked a demonstration which lasted for one hour and seventeen minutes. When his name was placed in nomination the next day, a flock of white doves was released and the birds circled round and round the hall before settling in a high open space in the center of the auditorium. When the first ballot was counted, using new automatic adding machines, Bryan was the choice of 892 delegates. The next closest candidate received only 59 votes.

For the third time in his amazing career, William Jennings Bryan had been nominated for President of the United States. The only two men to have previously received such an honor were Henry Clay and Grover Cleveland.

Now the overwhelming choice of the Democratic party, Bryan and his followers were certain that nothing could keep them from victory over the Republican nominee, William H. Taft. Even Alton Parker, the 1904 nominee, proclaimed, ''I am going to support the ticket of Bryan and Kern, and I want my friends to do the same thing.'' This was to be the year of the Commoner.

13
Keeping the Party in the Hands of Commoners

The Sunday morning following his third nomination for the presidency, William Jennings Bryan stood before a Sunday school class of adult Bible students in the country church near Fairview and led a discussion of the story of Saul and David. He regularly taught the class when he was home, and he didn't see why that should change when he became a candidate.

He gave his acceptance speech in Lincoln, something he had wanted to do in previous campaigns. It took as its theme "Shall the People Rule?" Bryan argued that the nation needed a government devoted to the protection of the common man rather than a government which was ruled by the rich. To accomplish this he called for direct election of senators and the publication of campaign contributions. He had already announced that any gifts to his campaign over $100.00 would be published each day, and that he would accept no money from corporations.

This time the leaders of the Bryan campaign agreed that he would make a series of key speeches devoted to major issues but would not undertake the free-wheeling travel schedule of the previous two election years. In Topeka, Kansas, he delivered a speech on the guarantee of bank deposits. At Indianapolis he spoke against the trusts to a wildly cheering crowd. On Labor Day he was in Chicago speaking to thousands of workers on topics where organized labor and the Democratic party were in agreement: the eight-hour work day, and the establishment of a Cabinet-level Department of Labor.

With those speeches over, Bryan grew restless and once again set out on an unrestricted speaking schedule. In the East he was welcomed in a fashion unheard of in Democratic politics. At the New York Democratic convention he stood on the platform clasping hands with Alton Parker as the thousands of delegates cheered. Bryan used new technology, as he had earlier with the phonograph. His people made a movie of the Labor Day address and sent a phonograph record along with it so they could be played at the same time. Talking pictures had not yet come into existence.

Faced with the prospect of a Bryan presidency, Roosevelt and others encouraged Taft to give up the traditional "front porch" campaign and to begin giving some speeches himself. Soon the crowds coming to hear Taft were reported to be as big as the audiences Bryan was drawing. When John D. Rockefeller and Andrew Carnegie endorsed the candidacy of Taft, Bryan delcared that this proved the Republican was in alliance with the big trusts. "Mr. Taft today is heading an army that has in it every financial pirate, every trust magnate," he told audiences from New York to Nebraska, "and I have not one single man who has his hand in another man's pocket. I appeal to the people who have been the victims of these men.''

On election night the scene at Fairview was familiar to those who had been through the previous two battles with Mr. Bryan. The porch was turned into a telegraph and newspaper office. Friends and neighbors dropped by to wish him well, and family members monitored the returns as they began to drift in. At first it appeared that they had finally accomplished their goal, but then the tide turned against Bryan. By 9:30 he announced that he was going to bed and would make no statement until morning. Ruth would not believe that her father had actually lost. She stayed up most of the night hoping the trend would change, but it didn't. William Howard Taft won the election, by a popular majority of more than one million people.

People offered many reasons why Bryan was defeated a third time. But the best explanation was the people had been thrilled with the two terms of President Roosevelt and they were willing to trust him to choose his own successor. They wanted four more years of what had been given to them by the popular ''Teddy.''

Once again Bryan returned to the lecture circuit. He was still the most sought after speaker in America. Traveling at times by wagon but more often by train and automobile, he followed the Chautauqua trail during the summer months and spoke at banquets and lyceum gatherings during the winter. Along with Mary and his two daughters, he traveled through Central and South America attending rounds of official receptions. Having been ordained as an elder by the Presbyterian church, he traveled to Edinburgh, Scotland, for a church-sponsored international peace meeting. Through the next several years he continued to keep his ideas before the people calling repeatedly for direct election of senators, an income tax, arbitration treaties between nations, and the national prohibition of liquor.

Bryan had always been a teetotaler, one who did not use liquor himself. When he was a very small boy he had signed the "pledge" at temperance meetings, promising that liquor would never pass his lips. However, for many years he had not felt that a national prohibition was necessary. He thought each city or county or state could decide for itself whether or not liquor should be sold within its boundaries. As more and more cities and even states voted "dry" he began to realize that the "option" as it was called, was not going to work. There were too many ways to get around the law when a person could simply go to the next town or state to get their booze.

Some men were quite inventive in the way they circumvented the law. One grocer in a "dry" state began to sell huge amounts of eggs. He had always carried eggs in his store, but now people seemed to be standing in line to buy eggs. Police officers put a plain-clothes man in the line. When they broke open the eggs which he purchased, they found within each egg a small bottle of whiskey around which the shell had been carefully joined back together.

Mr. Bryan saw the terrible consequences that drunkenness had upon individuals and families. He saw broken homes and the cold and hungry children in families where the father drank. He heard the great Presbyterian evangelist, Billy Sunday, bring his message against liquor, called "Booze, or Get On The Water Wagon." He was particularly upset to see saloons placing temptation before young men, knowing the devastation drinking could bring to their lives.

Bryan joined with others in the call for national prohibition and was criticized by some who said that his position did not agree with his previous calls for states rights and personal freedom. But he had an answer. "Personal liberty is often curbed for the greater good," he said. "Laws are made to protect society against burglary, which run counter to a man's right to enjoy a burglar's kit and a dark lantern; laws against arson deprive the citizen of the right to strike a match and burn his neighbor's house. How willingly should the people give up the right to drink when they can, by that act, reclaim thousands of men and bring comfort to countless miserable homes."

When liquor forces threatened to destroy him politically if he came out in favor of prohibition, Bryan replied, "If the liquor interests can make good their threat to destroy me politically, my death will be a warning to fathers and mothers of the power of this foe to the home and to American life."

Some who had been friends of Bryan in earlier campaigns now denounced him for his stand on prohibition. The famous lawyer, Clarence Darrow, traveled to Nebraska to speak for what he claimed was "man's right to do anything he wanted to do." Mr. Darrow had been an ardent supporter of Bryan in previous years.

As the election of 1912 drew closer, the politics of the nation became more confused than at any previous time in history. William Howard Taft had not carried out the policies of his predecessor, Teddy Roosevelt. So when the Republicans nominated Taft for a second term, Roosevelt decided to form a third party and run for himself. He called it the Bull Moose Party. Since both men were still popular with parts of the party, the Republicans were split right down the middle.

The split in the Republicans meant that the

Democrats had their best chance in years of electing the man they nominated to the office of president. Mary Bryan and others urged her husband to run once more for the nomination, but he refused. "I am not a candidate," he told everyone, "but give me a chance to fight in the ranks for a progressive candidate and I will show that I have fought not for myself but for a cause."

The principles the party included in their platform each time he had run for president were more important to Bryan than his own political future. He was more interested in seeing those policies in place than he was in becoming president himself. Many people could not understand that, and all through the days before the convention they accused him of trying to get the party to nominate him once again. But when the Democrats offered to let him make the keynote speech, which would have given him a chance to rally the people behind him as he had done in 1896, he refused. When they offered to make him permanent Chairman, he refused. He even refused to be Chairman of the Resolutions Committee which would have meant giving a speech in support of the platform. He was content to simply serve on that committee and once again make sure that the party was dedicated to the principle of equality and justice for the common man.

When it came time for the convention in Baltimore, Maryland, no one knew who Bryan supported for the nomination. His good friend Champ Clark, the Speaker of the House of Representatives, was running and Nebraska was pledged to him. As a delegate from Nebraska, Bryan would be voting for him at least on the first ballot. Governor Judson Harmon of Illinois and Oscar Underwood, chairman of the House Ways and Means Committee, had a number of delegates pledged to them. Governor Woodrow Wilson of New Jersey was also a candidate.

Wilson had been president of Princeton University from 1902 to 1910 and Governor of New Jersey for only two years. During those two years, however, he had pushed a number of reforms through the legislature, including a corrupt-practices law and an employers' liability law. Both of these were seen as laws which worked to overcome the power of big corporations.

Bryan had become acquainted with Wilson at a dinner hosted by Rev. and Mrs. Charles T. Erdman. Mrs. Wilson was the daughter of a Presbyterian minister and had known the Erdmans for many years. When Rev. Erdman invited Mr. Bryan to speak at Princeton Theological Seminary, where he was the president, Mrs. Wilson and Mrs. Erdman decided to get the three families together for dinner.

From that time on Mr. Bryan followed the activities of Governor Wilson closely and in the pages of *The Commoner* praised him often for the good work he was doing in New Jersey. But the fact still remained that Champ Clark had been his follower and friend for many years and Nebraska's delegates were pledged to Clark.

The Baltimore Convention began. As the delegates gathered the Bryans were amazed to see that three of the richest men in the country were there, men who were heads of great corporations whose monopolies Bryan had been fighting all these years. And they were there as delegates: J.P. Morgan and August Belmont from New York, and Thomas Ryan as a representative from Virginia, where he owned a large piece of property.

Bryan had made it very clear in the pages of *The Commoner* that he would not support anyone who had the approval of big businessmen from the East. He had seen how the railroads owned the politicians in Nebraska when he first came there. He believed that these businessmen would own anyone who got into office with their support and particularly with their money. So just before the voting for nominations began, he decided to make it impossible for these men to control the convention in any way.

"I would like to present a resolution to the convention," Bryan announced from his place on the floor in the middle of the Nebraska delegates.

As he walked onto the platform his appearance was greeted with widespread applause. These people had made him their candidate for president three times and they still loved him.

As Bryan read the resolution he had written out the night before, some of the cheers changed to boos. "We hereby declare ourselves opposed to the nomination of any candidate for president who is the representative of, or under obligation to, J. Pierpont Morgan, Thomas F. Ryan, August Belmont, or any other member of the privilege-hunting and favor-seeking class," he read. All over the auditorium people gasped. Those three men were sitting right among the delegates in front of him and he had the courage to call out their names. But Bryan wasn't finished. "Be it further resolved, that we demand the withdrawal from this convention of any delegate or delegates constituting or representing the above named interests." He was actually asking the convention to banish Morgan, Ryan, and Belmont and make them leave before the nominations began.

Immediately several men rushed to the platform and began shouting at Bryan that he was trying to destroy the Party. The entire room shook with people yelling against and in favor of Bryan's resolution.

Finally order was restored and when Bryan agreed to withdraw the last half of the resolution, the part that threw the men out of the convention, the resolution passed by a vote of 883 to 201. Satisfied that the Eastern business interests would not control the party, Bryan took his seat in the Nebraska delegation once again.

On the first ballot Nebraska voted for Clark, who ended up with the most votes. Wilson was second but neither man had enough votes to win the nomination. Another ballot was taken and then a third, but very few people changed their votes and still no one had enough to win. Six more ballots were taken with no change.

Then on the tenth ballot the New Yorkers, including Morgan and Belmont, switched their 90 votes from Harmon to Clark. Champ Clark suddenly jumped way ahead of Wilson and it looked almost certain that he would be the nominee of the Democratic party. While they were preparing for the next ballot, Bryan's brother Charles came back to the Nebraska delegation with a report of a secret agreement between the New York delegation and Champ Clark. They would support him for the nomination if he would remember his obligation to them when he became president. He would become the captive of the big business and trust forces, the very thing Bryan had been working so hard to avoid.

Still not sure that this "secret agreement" was actually in place, the Nebraska delegation kept voting for Clark. They thought that perhaps after one or two ballots the New Yorkers would switch their vote to Underwood who was really more to their liking. But the New York delegation kept voting for Clark. In spite of the fact that Champ Clark denied it, Bryan became convinced that the secret agreement really did exist.

As the fourteenth ballot was taken and the state of Nebraska was called, W.J. Bryan asked for permission to address the entire convention once again.

"I want to explain my vote," he told the chairman. "I withhold my vote from Mr. Clark as long as New York's vote is recorded for him. And the position that I take in regard to New York I will take in regard to any other candidate whose name is now or may be before the convention. I will cast my vote for Nebraska's second choice, Governor Wilson."

As a result of Bryan's decision the entire convention was thrown into an uproar. The balloting continued all that day and the next. When Champ Clark traveled up from Washington, D.C., to try and address the convention and explain his position, he found that they had all adjourned for the weekend. On the following Monday the balloting began again as twenty and then twenty-five and then thirty ballots were taken without a winner. But on the thirtieth ballot, Wilson moved passed Clark and became the front-runner.

Finally on the forty-sixth ballot, the Democrats nominated Woodrow Wilson to be their candidate for president. Bryan was satisfied that he had kept the corporations from controlling the party. It was still in the hands of the common man.

14
Peace Efforts

Once Woodrow Wilson was nominated by the Democrats, W.J. Bryan took to the stump as if he were running for president himself. For seven weeks he spoke constantly, averaging ten speeches a day. Since Wilson was running against both Taft and Roosevelt, it was a year of wild campaigning. Wilson, speaking on his own behalf, traveled the country giving a series of speeches which were later made into a book called *The New Freedom*. Roosevelt, an accomplished speaker in his own right, called his program the "New Nationalism." President Taft relied mainly on others to travel and speak for him since he was still in the White House and had the duties of the president to fulfill.

On October 14, 1912, a saloon keeper by the name of John N. Schrank shot Roosevelt just before he was to make a speech in Milwaukee, Wisconsin. An eyeglass case in Roosevelt's pocket deflected the bullet and saved his life. Although he was wounded, he insisted on giving the scheduled speech. Schrank was captured and committed to a mental institution.

Toward the end of the campaign Wilson came to

visit the Bryans in Lincoln. Thousands of Nebraskans met him at the train depot and cheered wildly as the motorcade carrying Wilson and Bryan traveled slowly through the streets toward the Lindell Hotel. There a banquet in honor of the candidate was held, with Bryan introducing Wilson as "a worthy leader of the great democratic forces of the nation." The next day they attended services at the Bryan's home church, Westminster Presbyterian, after which the members held a reception for them.

In addition to his speeches in support of Wilson, Bryan campaigned for other men on the Democratic ticket. In Missouri he campaigned for Champ Clark who was running for re-election to the House of Representatives. On the last full day of the campaign he gave nineteen speeches, the final one at the Omaha Auditorium.

As the election returns started to come in and it became obvious that Wilson was going to win, Bryan went before the crowd at the Lindell Hotel in Lincoln to tell them, "I am happier than Governor Wilson. I have confidence in him because I believe he listens to his conscience. Mr. Wilson is free to be a people's president."

When all the votes were counted, Wilson had defeated both Roosevelt and Taft. In the electoral college he received 435 votes to 88 for Roosevelt and only 8 for Taft. The principles for which Bryan had fought for all those years were going to be put into place, although he would not be the one in the White House leading the fight.

On December 21 the Bryans were invited to dinner at the governor's house in New Jersey. As they were eating, Mr. Wilson asked Mr. Bryan to become the Secretary of State in his new cabinet. Both Mary and her husband were pleased with the offer, but they

knew there were some questions which would have
to be settled first.

"You know the position I have always taken on the
use of alcohol," said Bryan. "Mrs. Bryan and I have
discussed this matter and we do not feel it would be
advisable to violate that custom even in the State
Department. I realize it has long been the custom at
state dinners to serve liquor, but we would not want
to do that if I were Secretary of State."

"That will be fine," answered the President-elect.
"I certainly believe that is a matter for you and Mrs.
Bryan to decide for yourselves."

"Thank you, Mr. Wilson. I certainly do not want
to do anything that would prove an embarrassment
at state functions, so I thought it best to get this matter
of alcohol settled before I accept your offer." Then
Mr. Bryan went on to his second matter of concern.
"You know that I have also for many years been
advocating the negotiation of a peace treaty among
all the nations of the world. In this treaty they would
agree to submit any disagreement to an impartial
tribunal who would decide the matter without anyone
going to war. If I were to be appointed Secretary of
State I would want to actively pursue that goal."

Bryan handed Wilson a copy of the proposed treaty,
and after looking it over Mr. Wilson said he had no
objection to what Bryan proposed. "It is certainly to
the benefit of our nation and the entire world to work
for the peaceful solution to our problems."

Delighted with the prospect of serving in
Washington as part of the government once again,
Mary and her husband moved from Fairview to the
capital in time for the inauguration of President
Wilson. As the cabinet stood behind him in front of
the Capitol Building, the new President took the oath
of office and gave his inaugural address. When he was

finished the crowd of more than 100,000 began to chant "Bryan, Bryan, Bryan. We want a speech from Bryan." The new Secretary of State turned away embarrassed and went to join his wife.

During the inaugural parade that followed, Mrs. Bryan rode with her husband in the carriage, and all along the route there was cheering and applause as people recognized the Commoner. Turning to Mrs. Bryan he said, "It is worth sixteen years of hard work to have devotion like this, isn't it?"

Settling into a number of rooms called the "Presidential Suite" at the Willard Hotel, Mr. and Mrs. Bryan began the process of meeting the various ambassadors with whom he would be working during his term as Secretary of State. The first important occasion was a diplomatic luncheon in honor of Ambassador and Mrs. Bryce from England who were returning home.

When the guests were all seated, Mr. Bryan rose and asked them to allow him to share a few words before the luncheon began.

"When the President asked me to become his Secretary of State," Mr. Bryan began, "I asked him whether taking that office would make it necessary for me to serve liquor, and he replied that he would leave that up to my own judgment. I have always been a teetotaler like my father before me, and I could not depart from the custom without contradicting my past. Please allow us to show our hospitality in other ways and pardon us if we omit the wines with your meal this evening."

After Bryan's speech the guests all applauded and the dinner began. With the meal the Bryans served white rock water and grape juice and everyone seemed completely satisfied with the arrangement. The Russian ambassador confided to his dinner partner that he had heard the new Secretary might not serve liquor, so he had taken a good drink before he arrived.

Although the Bryans were criticized by many people for not serving wine, others approved heartily. The wife of Vice-President Thomas Marshall soon announced that no wine would be served at any of her functions either. When other hostesses invited the Bryans to their dinners they were always careful to serve them grape juice, water, or even pineapple juice, while the other guests had their champagne.

The new Secretary of State made it his first priority to turn the State Department back to the common man. "It is impossible for a man to accept the post of ambassador unless he is rich," he wrote to President Wilson. "The government should build and furnish homes for ambassadors to other countries so that men who are qualified could be appointed whether or not they are rich." To Bryan's delight this proposal met the approval of both the President and Congress and became the regular practice of the United States diplomatic corps.

Bryan's greatest achievements, in his own opinion, were the many peace treaties he was able to sign with other nations. Starting with El Salvador on August 7, 1913, he made agreements with twenty-nine nations including England, France, and Italy. More and more nations promised to submit their differences to negotiators rather than going to war. The instrument of arbitration was to be the Permanent Court of Arbitration in the Hague, Netherlands, commonly called the Hague Court.

Excited about the prospects for world peace, Bryan ordered some old swords melted down and cast into small plow-shaped paperweights. On each plow was writtten the words from Isaiah 2:4, "They shall beat their swords into plowshares." Then he gave one of the souvenirs to each diplomat with whom he had worked to negotiate the treaties.

Columbia refused to sign a treaty with Mr. Bryan because they were still upset with the role the United States had played in the secession of Panama from Columbia. The Columbian ministry requested negotiations, and Bryan agreed. In an unprecendented action the Wilson government apologized to Columbia and promised to pay $25 million in settlement of Columbian claims against the United States. Teddy Roosevelt was outraged because while he was President he was the one who had encouraged Panama to secede. He succeeded in getting the Senate to refuse to ratify the treaty, but now everyone realized that the "Big Stick" days of the Roosevelt administration were over. Roosevelt once said he would "speak softly and carry a big stick," but Bryan wrote, "the man who speaks softly does not need a big stick."

In relation to the Philippines where Bryan had long advocated independence, he at first found President Wilson hesitant. But finally he prevailed upon him to support a bill that would promise the islands their independence, and the Jones Bill, as it was called, passed in 1916.

Two Constitutional Amendments which had been favorite principles of Bryan through the years were also ratified soon after he became Secretary of State. The Sixteenth Amendment which allowed the government to enact an income tax became law on February 15, 1913. That same year on May 31 the Seventeenth Amendment was also ratified. This one called for the direct election of senators instead of their appointment by the state legislatures. Bryan had included those two ideas in each of the platforms he wrote for the Democrats for sixteen years, and he was very happy to see them accepted by the nation.

Because of his constant effort on behalf of the direct election of senators, he was one of the signers of that document when it became a part of the Constitution of the United States.

In spite of the Secretary of State's firm commitment to peace, forces at work in Europe were not going to allow him or anyone else to succeed. On June 18, 1914, an heir to the Austrian throne known as Archduke Ferdinand was killed by a Serbian nationalist, and Austria declared war on Serbia. When Russia came to the help of Serbia, Germany entered on the side of Austria. Soon all of Europe was involved in what became known as the Great War.

Thousands of Americans were visiting Europe when the war broke out, and the State Department was busy for the first several weeks helping all of them to return safely to their homes. At the same time, Bryan began to work toward restoring peace in Europe. He convinced President Wilson to set aside a day of prayer when people could gather in churches to pray for peace. On that day he gave a speech in which he proclaimed, " 'Thou shalt not kill' applies to nations as well as to individuals."

When Oscar Straus, the United States member of the Hague Tribunal, brought him word that the German government would accept mediation if other nations would do the same, Bryan did his best to get Britain and France to agree to meet. President Wilson agreed that the United States would serve as the mediator if the other nations wanted that. But France refused to talk to Germany as long as German soldiers were on French soil. So the war continued.

Early in 1915 President Wilson decided to send a representative of the American government to the different nations of Europe on a peace mission. Secretary of State Bryan wanted desperately to make

such a trip and had offered many times to do so if
the President would let him. Instead, Wilson chose
a close friend by the name of Colonel Edward House.
Bryan was disappointed because he believed that
Colonel House was on the side of the British in the
war and would not remain neutral in his negotiations.

As the war continued in Europe it was inevitable
that the United States would be affected. Both sides
had declared that passengers of neutral countries could
not be kept safe if they insisted on traveling aboard
ships that flew the flags of the countries which were
at war. Secretary Bryan begged the President to issue
a warning limiting American travel to only those ships
which flew the United States flag, but he refused to
do so.

Although no one in the United States was suggesting that they become involved in the war in Europe, there were differing opinions as to how we should maintain our neutrality. Some members of Wilson's Cabinet thought it would be fine for American banks to lend money to the French government to fund their war efforts. Bryan argued that if we were going to be neutral we should not lend money to either side.

Then on May 7, 1915, the British ship *Lusitania* was sunk by German submarines and 1,198 people died, including 218 Americans. All across the nation people began calling on President Wilson to declare war on Germany. The President wrote a strong note to Germany protesting their action and requesting that they stop their submarine attacks on ships carrying Americans.

In response to those who were calling for war, Bryan pointed out that the British were actually trying to protect their munitions shipments by putting them on ships which were also carrying passengers. He thought that was like "putting women and children in front of an army." But the sentiment in favor of war, spurred on by men like Theodore Roosevelt, was too strong.

The reply from Germany to President Wilson's request to end submarine attacks was unsatisfactory. They made no promise of any kind, but instead left the door open to attack any ship of any nation with whom they were at war. So the President planned to send a second note. This was to make it very clear that the United States would demand "strict accountability" of Germany if they refused to halt the submarine warfare. Bryan felt that this would give Germany an opportunity to push the United States into the war even if they didn't want to get involved. If Germany continued submarine warfare, the United States would have to make them accountable for their actions and that could only mean war.

Bryan did not feel that he could continue as Secretary of State if the nation went to war so he sent his resignation to President Wilson with the explanation that it was to take effect when the second *Lusitania* note was sent to the German government. He also thought that when his followers across the nation learned that he had resigned they would convince President Wilson by letters and telegrams that the nation was in favor of peace instead of war.

When news of the Secretary of State's resignation became public the immediate reaction was one of outrage. Newspapers accused him of being disloyal and of deserting the President at a time when he was needed the most. But there were also many who supported his continued efforts toward peace. When early the next year Germany promised to abandon its unrestricted submarine warfare it looked again like the United States would be able to remain neutral in the war. Although Bryan did not attend the Democratic convention of 1916 as a delegate, he was in the press box when President Wilson was renominated with the slogan, "He kept us out of war."

After Wilson's nomination the crowd clamored to hear from Bryan and he spoke impromptu for an hour, praising Wilson because "he does not want this nation plunged into war." After his speech was over every delegate in the convention hall lined up to shake his hand.

15

Success for Prohibition and Women's Suffrage

The Republican nominee to oppose President Wilson in 1916 was Charles Evans Hughes, a former governor of New York and Supreme Court Justice. Since the Republicans were not divided by Roosevelt's Bull Moose Party this time, the Democrats realized they would have a much harder time winning than they had four years earlier. W.J. Bryan went to work for President Wilson in the way he knew best, giving speeches, particularly in the South and West where the President's support was the weakest. In addition to campaigning for the President, he worked hard for the cause of prohibition. Many states were voting on the liquor issue supported by the Webb-Kenyon Act of 1913 which made it illegal to ship liquor from a wet state to a dry state.

Along with Evangelist Billy Sunday, Bryan was prohibition's greatest orator. Many times the two men shared the same platform. Sunday would speak first, wrestling with the devil, breaking chairs across the pulpit, stamping on the platform until the nails gave way and the boards bulged up, all the while running and shouting out his attack on the evils of "booze." Then would come Bryan who stood almost still on the platform, a huge block of ice in front of him which he periodically wiped with a handkerchief for cooling his face. Only occasionally did he gesture with one hand, but his voice was as powerful as Billy Sunday's gymnastics.

"Rise," he would invite the audience, "and let us pledge our support to the cause in water. It ascends from the seas, obedient to the summons of the sun, and descending, showers blessings upon the earth. It gives beauty to the fragrant flowers; its alchemy transmutes base clay into golden grain; it is the canvas upon which the finger of the infinite traces the radiant rainbow of promise. It is the drink that refreshes and adds no sorrow with it. Jehovah looked upon it at creation's dawn and said: 'It is good'."

Bryan also campaigned for the right of women to vote. "I shall claim no privilege for myself that I do not ask for my wife," he said. "Since man trusts woman everywhere else; why not at the polls? If men learn most of what they know about government from women schoolteachers does that not create a presumption for women's suffrage?"

But his greatest theme was peace, and his entire campaign for Wilson was based on the theme of the convention, "He kept us out of war." Touring across nineteen states during the course of the election campaign, he told listeners everywhere, "I join the people in thanking God that we have a President who does not want the nation to fight."

As expected, the election was very close, but Wilson won with 49.4 percent of the vote. Of the nineteen states where Bryan campaigned, fourteen went for Wilson. Even more significant was the fact that seventeen of the twenty-three states which were now "dry," having voted in state-wide prohibition, also supported the President.

The President kept his campaign promises concerning peace by appealing to all the warring nations to state the terms on which the war could be ended and offering to serve as the mediator. Bryan was thrilled when he heard the news because that was exactly what he had tried to get President Wilson to do while he was the Secretary of State. However, when the appeal was delivered in Europe, the warring countries refused.

In a speech before the Senate on January 22, 1917, President Wilson continued his quest for peace. He called for a League of Nations to establish world peace, another one of Bryan's ideas from the past. But the response to this was even worse than the response to his earlier offer to mediate the conflict. Now Germany announced that she would reopen unrestricted submarine warfare and any merchant ship found in the war zone would be sunk. President Wilson no doubt remembered that in the second *Lusitania* letter, which Bryan had refused to sign, he had said he would break off relations with Germany if the submarine warfare was resumed. On February 2 he reluctantly did so.

W.J. Bryan immediately issued "An Appeal for Peace to the American People" outlining the steps through which the nation could avoid war. Telegrams asking Senators and Congressmen to support Mr. Bryan's proposals poured into Washington. He traveled extensively, speaking at the District of Columbia Anti-War League meeting, Madison Square Garden and many other stops but the progress toward war could not be stopped.

Merchant ships, which were the primary means of carrying goods at that time, began to stack up in the nation's harbors. President Wilson decided that American merchant ships should be armed to defend themselves. A letter was discovered, written by the German Foreign Secretary Alfred Zimmerman, which called for an alliance of Mexico and Japan against the United States. As the newly armed merchant ships set out for foreign ports, Germany sank three of them with her U-boats. On April 2 President Wilson asked Congress to recognize that a state of war existed between the United States and Germany.

As he had once before during the Spanish American War, Bryan yielded immediately to the decision of his government. He sent a telegram to President Wilson, "Please enroll me as a private whenever I am needed and assign me to any work that I can do." Although he knew he was too old for his offer to be considered, he wanted the nation to know that he was still a patriot. He would work for peace as long as peace was possible, but when his nation decided war was necessary he was ready to fight.

During the war Bryan continued to travel and speak, promoting war bonds and Liberty Loans. "Let's play Garden Golf," he told his audiences. "The victory gardener wielding his hoe can help our boys win the war. Your ice chest is the nineteenth hole and the game is won by the one driving home the most potatoes." As Nebraska boys marched off to war they stopped at Lincoln and marched to the hotel for dinner where fifty young girls dressed as Red Cross workers pinned a flower on each one. Then Bryan spoke to them in the City Auditorium telling them what a privilege it was to fight for freedom and democracy.

The two favorite themes on which Bryan spoke during the war were prohibition and women's suffrage. He saw in the progress of the war several strong reasons why the nation should accept prohibition: "Grain must not be wasted in alcohol; victory gardens will do little to help if seven million acres are devoted to growing grain for drink, and the fighting men need clear brains and steady nerves."

The crusade against the Demon Drink was almost like another presidential campaign. Since many states were still voting on state-wide prohibition, Bryan was invited to visit those states and speak in favor of outlawing the saloons. Just as during the days when he was running for president, a crowd would meet him at the depot, there would be a parade through the streets, and an audience of thousands would applaud and cheer his oratory. "A city would not license the establishment of a rifle range in a public park even if it could be assured that no more than one passerby in one thousand would be killed by a stray bullet," he told them. "But the percentage killed by drink is greater than that."

In December of 1917 his work was rewarded. He sat in the press gallery of the House of Representatives as they voted in favor of the Eighteenth Amendment to the Constitution of the United States prohibiting the "manufacture, sale or transportation of intoxicating liquors." After celebrating that step by Congress, he set to work speaking again to convince the individual states to ratify the amendment. In March of 1918 he was elected president of the National Dry Federation which included twenty-eight different national groups.

Encouraged by their success in the area of prohibition, Bryan and others worked even harder for the right of women to vote. "It is presumed," he said to one of his audiences in New York, "that when a man has confidence enough in a woman to give himself to her, that he ought to have confidence enough in her to give her the ballot." In response to Bryan and many others, Congress passed the Nineteenth Amendment to the Constitution. This amendment said, "The right of citizens of the United States to vote shall not be denied or abridged by the United States or by any State on account of sex."

Even though Bryan was not the president, it seemed as if all the principles he had supported for many years were being adopted. As he traveled across the nation on the Chautauqua circuit, he was as popular as he had ever been with the common people. One audience which was scheduled to hear him at 8:00 P.M. waited until after midnight for him to show up. He had run into problems with a train car which had jumped the track. But even after midnight they still wanted him to speak and they stayed and listened until 2:00 A.M., cheering everything he said.

Bryan was still concerned about the war which raged in Europe. With great joy he heard news of the

Armistice which was signed on November 11, 1918. When President Wilson traveled to Europe for the peace negotiations, he carried with him a plan which called for the establishment of a League of Nations. This League would require a one-year delay in any dispute before war could be declared and a special investigating commission to help settle disputes. Both of these were ideas that Bryan had been promoting for more than twenty years in his peace treaties.

The League of Nations met with opposition in the Senate and in spite of great effort on the part of the President and Mr. Bryan, the treaty was not ratified by the Senate, and the League of Nations did not become a reality.

Success came in several other areas, however, to offset that disappointment. States quickly ratified the Prohibition Amendment with Nebraska being the thirty-sixth state to do so and therefore the one which accomplished its final passage. The dry forces called for a big party to celebrate the passing of America from the wet era. Bryan was the principal speaker. For the theme of his speech, he used a Bible text: "They are dead which sought the young child's life."

"Since King Alcohol has slain a million times as many children as King Herod did," he told the huge party gathering, "no words could be more appropriate than these to describe the passing of the saloon from the American scene."

When in August of 1920 the Nineteenth Amendment, allowing women to vote, was also ratified by the states, Bryan rejoiced. At his sixtieth birthday party he told the crowd, "My faith is even greater now since I have seen reform after reform accomplished and great principles that were at first scoffed at, written into the unrepealable law of the land."

During the war the Bryans moved to Florida, and purchased a home they called Villa Serena. There they joined the First Presbyterian Church of Miami, and Mr. Bryan was invited to teach a men's Sunday school class. Soon the class outgrew the church building and they moved to the Royal Palm park in Coral Gables where he taught from under a bandshell. As many as five thousand men gathered each Sunday to hear him teach from the Word of God. Almost every Sunday some stayed after class to talk with Mr. Bryan about how to begin the Christian life.

When he was invited by the International Young Men's Christian Association to help them begin work in Canada, he and Mary set off on a speaking tour of a different sort. They traveled across Canada on the Western Canadian Pacific starting in British Columbia and moving east. Each night found them in a new town and meeting with local people interested in starting a branch of the YMCA.

At the dedication of a new YMCA building in Indianapolis Mr. Bryan spoke on "My Yoke Is Easy," and seventeen boys came forward to be converted. From there he went to speak in a Methodist college where one of the teachers told him that she had been a missionary in Japan during the Bryans' visit to that country and that ten Japanese boys out of a class of thirteen had accepted Christ after reading his speech on "The Prince of Peace."

With most of his political battles behind him, Mr. Bryan turned to a matter which had long concerned him, the question of evolution. He developed a new speech called "The Menace of Darwinism" in which he declared that "all morality and virtue depend on religion and belief in God. We cannot afford to have the faith of our children undermined."

When he discovered that evolution was being taught

in public schools all across the nation, Bryan began taking his fight against Darwinism to the state legislatures, just as he had done with prohibition. One of the first states to pass a law against the teaching of evolution was the state of Kentucky. When he was invited to speak to the state legislators there, he condemned the ''teaching of irreligion in our public schools and universities. If agnostics or atheists or unbelievers of any sort wish to teach their beliefs they should have the right to establish their own schools, but they should not be permitted to teach their ideas in schools maintained by public taxation.''

Following his speech the Kentucky legislature passed a bill making it illegal to teach evolution in the public schools of Kentucky. Mr. Bryan went on his way to speak in other states, not realizing he would soon return to Kentucky to fight the greatest battle yet against evolution.

16

The Famous Scopes Trial

When the Democrats held their national convention in New York City in 1924, W.J. Bryan attended as a delegate from Florida rather than Nebraska. His brother Charles, however, was now the governor of Nebraska and came to the convention as a member of that delegation. Once again Bryan helped to write the platform as he had done now for almost thirty years, and when John W. Davis was nominated on the 103rd ballot he chose Charles Bryan as his running mate. Bryan campaigned hard for his brother giving more than one hundred speeches, but President Calvin Coolidge, who had succeeded to the presidency on the death of President Harding, defeated them in the election.

With another election over, Bryan turned his attention once again to the question of evolution. He was convinced that the teachings of evolution concerning the survival of the fittest was one of the causes of the war which had just been fought in Europe. He blamed evolution for the conflicts which were going on in both church and school across the land. Modernists, who were taking over many religious denominations, also supported evolution, and while some of them taught that God worked through evolution, Bryan said, "Theistic evolution is an anesthetic; it deadens the pain while the Christian's religion is being removed. God didn't work through evolution, but through miracles."

Bryan's speeches against evolution were widely heard, as he traveled to churches and schools and continued to spend his summers on the Chautauqua circuit. He was constantly encouraged by his doctors to slow down because he had diabetes, but he found it hard to turn down any invitation to speak. The only thing that kept him from traveling even more was the ill health of Mary, who was suffering from arthritis and was now confined to a wheelchair. He still taught a weekly Sunday school class, and he wrote a syndicated column for newspapers called "Bible Talks." A compilation of his religious lectures titled, *In His Image*, became a best selling book.

Mr. Bryan also spoke before state legislatures who were, like Tennessee, considering bills to prohibit the teaching of evolution in public schools. "The hand that writes the pay check rules the school," he told the legislature of West Virginia. The basic issue was whether or not a state which paid for public education had the right to decide what was taught in its schools. Bryan thought they had every right to decide.

On April 25, 1925, a group of men in a small town in Tennessee called Dayton were talking about the anti-evolution law which the Tennessee Legislature had just passed. A lawyer by the name of Hicks, Superintendent White of the local school system, and a man named Rappelyea came up with the idea of testing the new law right there in Dayton.

John Scopes had been teaching science in Dayton High School that year as well as coaching, and everyone liked him, but the men thought it might be a good way to put their town on the map. Besides, the American Civil Liberties Union had already agreed to pay the expenses of any teacher who was tried under the new law, so it wouldn't cost Scopes anything. A student was sent off to find Scopes, who was playing tennis at the high school, and soon he arrived at Robinson's Drug Store where the men were talking.

"John," said Mr. Rappelyea to the young teacher, "do you think it's possible to teach biology without teaching evolution?"

"Not in this state," answered Scopes promptly. "The official, state-approved biology textbook, Hunter's *Civic Biology*, teaches evolution."

Since the drug store also sold textbooks, someone grabbed the book John Scopes mentioned and sure enough, it talked about evolution just like he said.

"So, John," went on Mr. Rappelyea, "did you teach evolution at Dayton High School this last year?"

"Well, I substituted for Mr. Ferguson a couple of days, if that's what you mean."

"And used this textbook?"

"Well, sure. That's the book he was using."

"Then you've been violating the law," said lawyer Hicks. "You ought to be arrested."

"Wait a minute," answered Scopes. "If I've been violating the law so has every other science teacher. That's the text used all over the state. What are you fellows trying do to, anyway?"

When the men explained the A.C.L.U. was looking for a test case so they could try to overturn the law, Scopes was reluctant. But as they continued to explain that it wouldn't cost him anything, he finally agreed,

"If you can prove that I've taught evolution and that I can qualify as a defendant, then I'll be willing to stand trial."

Mr. Rappelyea headed over to the telegraph office to send out a telegram to the A.C.L.U., John Scopes went back to his tennis game and the rest of the men went home for supper, not realizing they had started what would become one of the most famous trials of the century. Two days later, when they had a telegram from the A.C.L.U. which agreed to take the case, they decided the teacher should probably be arrested, and Scopes himself went out to find a deputy sheriff who could serve the papers. On April 9 he appeared before three local justices of the peace who bound him over to a grand jury.

When the story appeared in the newspapers, W.J. Bryan was in the middle of one of his speaking tours. Dr. William Bell Riley, pastor of the First Baptist Church of Minneapolis and president of the World Christian Fundamentals Association, suggested to Bryan that he volunteer to serve as a lawyer in the case against John Scopes. Bryan agreed that he would do so if the local prosecuting lawyers approved. When Mr. Hicks, the lawyer from Dayton, saw that in the paper he immediately wired Mr. Bryan inviting him to join him and his brother in the prosecution.

The A.C.L.U. in the meantime had secured the services of a lawyer by the name of Clarence Darrow. Darrow was a friend and supporter of Bryan from his early election campaigns. He was a successful trial lawyer who enjoyed taking cases that no one else wanted. His most famous trial had been the defense of two young men named Loeb and Leopold, accused of murder. He was a brilliant debater, an opponent of punishment for crime, and a religious agnostic.

When the trial began on July 10 it seemed to

Dayton residents as if the entire world were watching.
WGN Radio from Chicago broadcast the trial direct
from the courtroom. More than one hundred reporters
were in town representing all the large news services
and several foreign countries. In addition to Bryan
and Darrow there were other lawyers involved, like
William Jennings Bryan, Jr., from California and
Dudley Malone, who had once been Bryan's assistant
when he was Secretary of State but was now helping
Clarence Darrow on the defense team.

There was also a motley collection of strangers in
town, like a bearded man who announced that he was
"John the Baptist the Third" and Deck Carter, the
"Bible Champion of the World," who claimed to be
the only person since Joan of Arc to whom God had
spoken directly. Some reporters, looking for stories
to send back to their newspapers, interviewed these
people and made it sound as if they were typical of
all the fundamentalists in Dayton.

Every seat was taken and people were standing in
every available space as the trial got under way. Word
spread through the crowd that this was the
twenty-ninth anniversary of Mr. Bryan's "Cross of
Gold" speech, and when he entered the courtroom
he was greeted by long and enthusiastic applause "in
honor of the anniversary." The judge soon discovered
that he would have to put a stop to all applause or
they would never get through the trial. After
photographers took pictures of all the lawyers and
everyone greeted each other, the judge called for
attention and announced that one of the local ministers
would open the courtroom session with prayer.

The first few days of the trial were rather dull as
the jury was selected and the charges were read. When
the weekend came Bryan was in great demand as a
speaker in area churches. He taught Sunday school
at the Methodist Church and then addressed a large
audience on the courthouse lawn that afternoon.
During that speech he denied that he was trying to
put "God into the Constitution. Our purpose," he
said, "is to vindicate the right of parents to guard the
religion of their children against efforts made in the
name of science to undermine faith in supernatural
religion. There is no attack on free speech, or freedom
of the press, or freedom of thought, or freedom of
knowledge, but surely parents have a right to guard

the religious welfare of their children.''

After almost a week there had still been no major speeches by either Darrow or Bryan. Four witnesses testified that John Scopes had taught evolution in the classroom at Dayton High School. It seemed obvious that this was in violation of the law which the Tennessee Legislature had passed. But the defense announced that they would prove that the law actually had two requirements. It said that evolution could not be taught and that the theory of Divine creation could not be denied. The defense was arguing that both parts of the law had to be broken before Scopes was guilty. They were going to prove that Scopes had not denied the theory of Divine creation. There were many people who believed in both creation and evolution, John Scopes among them.

As part of the defense they wanted to introduce the testimony of fifteen scientists and clergymen into the trial. This testimony was for the purpose of demonstrating that many people accepted both evolution and Divine creation. If they could prove that Scopes had broken only part of the law but not all of it then he would not be guilty.

The prosecution lawyers objected to the testimony of the scientists and clergymen who believed in evolution. They did not want the trial to center on what people believed about evolution. They wanted the judge to decide whether or not the law had actually been violated. As the arguments for and against allowing the experts to testify were given, Bryan rose to deliver a speech to the court.

''We do not need any expert to tell us what the law means,'' he said. ''This is not the place to try to prove that the law ought never to have been passed. The place to prove that was at the legislature. The people of this state knew what they were doing when they passed the law, and they knew the dangers of the doctrine—that they did not want it taught to their children. It isn't proper to bring experts in here to try to defeat the purpose of this state.''

''The point is that the law has been violated. There is the book from which they were teaching your children that man was a mammal and so indistinguishable among the mammals that they leave him there with thirty-four hundred and ninety-nine other mammals—including elephants.''

The crowd laughed when he said that, enjoying the wit and wisdom of the man they had been waiting to hear ever since the trial began. Picking up another book which had been sitting on the desk next to the

biology book, Bryan waved it in front of the crowd. "What is the logical end of the evolutionary theory?" he questioned them. "I have here a copy of Mr. Darrow's arguments in the Loeb-Leopold trial where he says that the teachings of Nietzsche who carried Darwinism to its logical conclusions made Leopold a murderer."

Clarence Darrow was on his feet immediately. "I object," he yelled. "Nietzsche never taught that."

"I will read what you said in that speech," replied Bryan, opening the small book which had been on sale all over Dayton. "Here it is on page eighty-four, and I read, 'It is hardly fair to hang a nineteen-year-old boy for the philosophy that was taught him at the university.' "

"But that is not all that I said," Mr. Darrow interrupted again. "Read the rest of it."

"I'll read the part I want and you read the rest," Bryan answered good-naturedly and the crowd responded with applause and laughter. They were glad to see their hero get the best of the big lawyer from Chicago.

"The facts are simple, the case is plain," he concluded, "and if those gentlemen want to enter upon a larger field of educational work on the subject of evolution, let us get through with this case and then convene a mock court, for it will deserve the title of mock court if its purpose is to banish from the hearts of the people the Word of God as revealed."

In response to Mr. Bryan's speech, Dudley Malone delivered a brilliant address in favor of freedom of speech and allowing the experts to testify. When he finished, Bryan turned to him and said, "Dudley, that was the greatest speech I ever heard."

On the second weekend of the trial Bryan was again busy speaking at various area churches. He traveled

to Chattanooga and Walden Ridge where about five
hundred people came to hear him preach.

The crowd in the courthouse was so large on
Monday that the judge was afraid the floor would
collapse, so he adjourned the entire court to the lawn
out front. There the defense, frustrated at not being
able to use the witnesses they had brought to town,
announced the great surprise of the trial. "The defense
desires to call Mr. Bryan as a witness," said a lawyer
by the name of Hays.

The rest of the prosecution lawyers objected
immediately. Even the judge was perplexed. It was
unheard of for a lawyer on one side of a case to call
a lawyer on the other side as a witness. But Bryan
was more than willing to testify. "If Your Honor
please, I insist that Mr. Darrow can be put on the
stand, and Mr. Malone and Mr. Hays," he told the
judge.

Finally Judge Raulston agreed and Mr. Darrow
stepped forward to begin questioning William
Jennings Bryan. "You have given considerable study
to the Bible, haven't you, Mr. Bryan?"

"Yes sir, I have tried to," Bryan answered.

For the next two hours he sat and answered
questions on every topic imaginable, many of which
had nothing to do with the trial itself. Under Darrow's
questioning he explained that although he believed
in a literal interpretation of the Bible there were figures
of speech like "Ye are the salt of the earth," which
could not be taken literally. He explained that it was
actually a great fish which had swallowed Jonah rather
than a whale and assured Mr. Darrow that he still
believed that miracle.

They talked about the long day of Joshua, and
Darrow launched into a long argument about how
such an event would have caused the earth to change

into a molten matter. But Bryan simply answered that
the same God who prolonged the day could take care
of any consequences which were a result of that
miracle. Then the lawyer went on to the story of the
Flood and the age of the earth and where Cain got
his wife, with side trips into the fields of history, com-
parative religion, anthropology, archaeology,
linguistics, and geology. In answer to each question,
while freely admitting that he had not studied all those
areas of science, Bryan defended his belief in the Word
of God.

Clarence Darrow was shrewd and he repeatedly
ridiculed Bryan for what he believed, saying that he
was trying to prevent "bigots and ignoramuses from
controlling the education of the United States."

Finally, exhausted from the unrelenting attack
under the hot afternoon sun, Bryan rose to his feet
and turned to the judge. "Your Honor, I think I can
shorten this testimony. The only purpose Mr. Darrow
has is to slur at the Bible. But I will shorten his
question. I will answer it all at once, and I have no
objection in the world, I want the world to know that
this man, who does not believe in God, is trying to
use a court in Tennessee . . ."

"I object to that!" Darrow interrupted loudly, but
Bryan continued in his most powerful voice.

"To slur it," he said. "And, while it will require
time, I am willing to take it."

"I object," Darrow shouted again. "I am
examining you on your fool ideas that no intelligent
Christian on earth believes."

Realizing that the defense had not really been trying
to submit evidence but was simply trying to make Mr.
Bryan look foolish, the judge adjourned the court until
the following morning. When they reconvened the
next morning the judge ordered Mr. Bryan's

testimony stricken from the record and he refused to allow the prosecution to examine Mr. Darrow and the other lawyers on the witness stand. Then the judge summed up the case for the jury declaring that the basic issue was whether or not Mr. Scopes taught that man descended from a lower order of animals. To the surprise of the prosecution, Mr. Darrow stood and agreed with the judge, in effect suggesting that his client should be found guilty of violating the Tennessee law. He was eager to get the case over so they could appeal the decision to a higher court.

The jury filed out and in eight minutes they were back with their verdict. John Scopes was guilty of teaching evolution. The judge fined him $100 and court costs and the lawyers began to work on his appeal. A final prayer was offered and the trial was over.

17

The Flag at Half-Mast for the Common People's Hero

William Bryan had hoped to give a closing speech at the trial in Dayton which would once and for all answer the question of evolution, but the abrupt end of the trial kept that from happening. Since he had worked on the speech for so long, he decided to have it put into print instead. He made arrangements with a printer in Chattanooga, and the Friday after the trial he traveled down there to check over the proofs. Also that day he visited a site in Dayton where a group of businessmen were planning to start the "first fundamentalist university in America." This later became known as Bryan College.

On Saturday the Bryans traveled to Winchester where they had been invited to visit Judge Raulston and his family. After dinner he was asked to give a speech to the one hundred or so people who had gathered for the luncheon in his honor. While friends took Mrs. Bryan back to Dayton, her husband returned to Chattanooga by train. Along the way he spoke to people who gathered at stations along the route, and reporters estimated that more than 50,000 people in all heard him speak during the one trip. In Chattanooga he received a medical checkup. The doctor told him he had several more years to live.

Sunday morning he was back in Dayton once again and was invited to lead in prayer during the service at the Methodist Church. After the service, nearly the entire congregation stayed around to shake his hand and congratulate him on the outcome of the trial. "It was a great victory for Christianity and a staggering blow to the forces of darkness," he said.

After arranging with the choir director the hymns which would be used in preparation for his sermon that evening, he and Mary returned for dinner to the house where they were staying. Bryan told his wife about the medical examination he had had in Chattanooga, assuring her that his blood pressure was suitable for his age, his heart action was normal and that the other tests were entirely satisfactory. They talked about plans for the future, including a tour to Bible lands with five hundred people he was preparing to lead. When dinner was over he made a few phone calls and then told Mary he was going to take a short nap on the side porch. Two hours later when they went to wake him they discovered that he had died in his sleep.

As word of Bryan's death spread through the city of Dayton, mourners by the hundreds began gathering. Farmers and their families, shopkeepers, mill workers and others came and stood in front of the small cottage where the "Commoner" lay. He was and would always be one of them. Ministers offered prayers, and hymns were sung quietly as people came and went for the next two days. Finally the body was placed on a train and several thousand people gathered at the station to say farewell.

Mrs. Bryan and the children decided that Washington was the place where Bryan should be buried. As the train traveled east, crowds gathered at every station, almost as if they were waiting for the familiar figure to appear on the back platform of the railroad car and begin speaking. At Jefferson City, Tennessee, a quartet of young men stood on a pile of railway ties and sang one of Bryan's favorite hymns, "One Sweetly Solemn Thought."

"The last journey was like the earlier campaigns," said Mary, "except that now there was sorrow on the faces that pressed around the windows. The great crowds of people were silent and no one came to the back platform to greet them."

In Washington, Bryan lay in state in the New York Avenue Presbyterian Church while 20,000 people filed by the casket. The White House flag was flown at half-mast and President Coolidge issued a statement of profound regret, adding in a note to Mary that "the sincerity of his motives was beyond dispute." Clarence Darrow told reporters that he had voted for Bryan twice and respected his "sincerity and devotion." Senator Ashurst of Arizona paid tribute to him, saying his "superlative oratory, his frame of oak, and his apostolic zeal brought the income tax, women's suffrage, prohibition and direct election of senators" to the nation.

Dr. Joseph Sizoo preached the funeral message, telling the audience that he had been called to the ministry through the influence of one of Bryan's addresses. He described Bryan as "a rebuilder of God's altar" in a message which was carried across the country by radio.

But it was the Rev. George Stuart who, in offering the final prayer at Arlington Cemetery, captured the true spirit of William Jennings Bryan's life. After the coffin was escorted to the grave by three companies of artillerymen, the Third Cavalry band played "Lead, Kindly Light." Then the bugler blew Taps, and finally Rev. Stuart prayed.

"We thank Thee," he said simply, "for this great hero of the common people."

And the body of the Great Commoner was laid to rest.

EVENTS IN THE LIFE OF WILLIAM JENNINGS BRYAN

1860   March 19, William Bryan is born in Salem, Illinois.

Abraham Lincoln is elected President of the United States.

1872   William's father, Silas Bryan, runs for the United States House of Representatives.

1873   Evangelist Dwight L. Moody holds his first revival campaign in England.

1874   Willy Bryan is converted in a revival service at the Cumberland Presbyterian Church in Salem.

1875   Bryan enters Whipple Academy in Jacksonville, Illinois.

1877   Bryan enrolls at Illinois College in Jacksonville.

1879   William Bryan meets Miss Mary Baird, a student at Jacksonville Female Academy.

1880   Silas Bryan dies.

1881   William Bryan graduates from Illinois College and enters Union College of Law in Chicago.

1883   After graduating from Union, Bryan opens a law office in Jacksonville.

1884   William Bryan attends the Democratic National Convention in Chicago which nominates Grover Cleveland for President.

On October 1, 1884 William is married to Mary Baird.

Grover Cleveland is elected President of the United States, the first Democrat since the Civil War to hold that office.

1887   The Bryans move to Lincoln, Nebraska, where William becomes a law partner of Adolph Talbot.

1888   William attends the Democratic National Convention in St. Louis, Missouri, which re-nominates Cleveland.

Benjamin Harrison defeats Cleveland in the election.

1890   Bryan is elected to the United States House of Representatives from the state of Nebraska.

1891   Bryan is appointed to the powerful Ways and Means Committee.

1892   Bryan is elected to a second term in the House.

Grover Cleveland defeats Benjamin Harrison in the presidential election.

1893   The United States experiences a deep recession called the Panic of 1893.

1894   President Cleveland sends federal troops to break up the Pullman Strike against the railroads.

Bryan becomes the editor of the Omaha *World Herald*.

1896   Bryan delivers his most famous speech, the "Cross of Gold" speech, and is nominated for President of the United States by the Democratic National Convention in Chicago.

William McKinley defeats Bryan in the presidential election.

1898   The Spanish-American War begins.

Bryan becomes a colonel and leads Nebraska's Third Regiment.

1900   Bryan is again nominated for president and again loses to William McKinley.

Bryan starts a weekly paper called *The Commoner*.

1901   President McKinley is assassinated and Theodore Roosevelt becomes President.

1904   Theodore Roosevelt is re-elected President.

1906 The Bryan family takes a trip around the world.
1908 Nominated for president for a third time, Bryan
      is defeated by William Howard Taft.
1912 Democrat Woodrow Wilson is elected President
      and invites Bryan to become his Secretary
      of State.
1913 The Sixteenth and Seventeenth Amendments
      to the Constitution are adopted allowing for
      income tax and the direct election of senators.
1914 War breaks out in Europe.
1915 Bryan resigns as Secretary of State.
1916 President Wilson is re-elected President on the
      slogan "He kept us out of war."
1917 The United States enters World War I on the
      side of the Allies.
1918 The war ends with the victory of the Allies.
1919 The Eighteenth Amendment to the Constitu-
      tion is ratified making Prohibition the law
      of the land.
1920 The Nineteenth Amendment, giving women
      the right to vote, is ratified.
      Warren Harding is elected President.
1924 Calvin Coolidge is elected President, defeating
      John W. Davis and his running mate Charles
      Bryan, William's brother.
1925 William Jennings Bryan joins the prosecution
      for the Scopes trial in Dayton, Tennessee,
      and sees him convicted of teaching evolution
      in a public school.
      Five days after the trial, Bryan dies in Dayton
      and is taken to Arlington National Cemetery
      for burial.

BIBLIOGRAPHY

Bryan, William J. and Mary. *The Memoirs of William Jennings Bryan*. 1925

Cherny, Robert A. *A Righteous Cause*. Boston: Little, Brown and Company, 1985.

Curtis, Richard K. *They Called Him Mister Moody*. Grand Rapids, Michigan: William B. Eerdmans Publishing Co., 1962.

de Camp, L. Sprague. *The Great Monkey Trial*. Garden City, New York: Doubleday and Co., 1968.

Gray, R. L. *Wit, Wisdom and Eloquence*. Atlanta: Harrison Co., 1930.

Glad, Paul W. *McKinley, Bryan and the People*. Philadelphia and New York: J.B. Lippincott Co., 1964.

Glad, Paul, W. *William Jennings Bryan*. New York: Hill and Wang, 1968.

Koenig, Louis W. *Bryan*. New York: G.P. Putnam's Sons, 1971.

Kosner, Alice. *The Voice of the People*. New York: Julian Messer Co., 1970.

Levine, Lawrence W. *Defender of the Faith*. New York: Oxford University Press, 1965.

Oliver, Robert T. *History of Public Speaking in America*. Boston: Allyn and Bacon, Inc., 1965.

Werner, M. R. *Bryan*. New York: Harcourt, Brace and Co., 1929.

INDEX

ABOUT THE AUTHOR

Robert Allen is the father of four children, Chad, Wendy, Kent and Tammy, who love to read his books and listen to his stories. Father and children together have produced a weekly radio program and children's tapes on which they are known as the Bible Story Family. Allen's retelling of the stories of great Old Testament kings has made him a popular speaker at Christian schools and summer camps. He also is known for his monodramas of great American speakers.

Mr. Allen heads the Speech Department at Pillsbury College in Owatonna, Minnesota, where he lives with his wife and family. There he seeks to train others who will help lead the nation through their speaking ability, as William Jennings Bryan did.

ABOUT THE ARTIST

Peggy Trabalka lives in historic Milford, Michigan. There she does what she loves most—turning stories into beautiful pictures. She is a member of galleries and artistic clubs and illustrates children's books. Peggy has a passion for art! She feels an illustration should be a personal experience. She comes from a long line of storytellers; she enjoys making history come alive.

An artist almost since birth, Peggy attended Cass Technical School to polish her skills. She makes her living as a free-lance commercial artist.